Child Exploitation

ISSUES

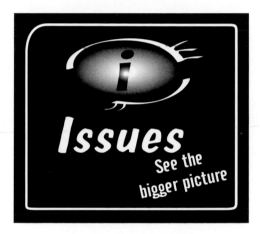

Volume 202

Series Editor

Lisa Firth

Independence

Educational Publishers

Cambridge

First published by Independence

The Studio, High Green

Great Shelford

Cambridge CB22 5EG

England

© Independence 2011

British Library Cataloguing in Publication Data
Child exploitation. – (Issues ; v. 202)

1. Child labor. 2. Child sexual abuse. 3. Child soldiers.

4. Exploitation.

I. Series II. Firth, Lisa.

331.3'1-dc22

ISBN-13: 978 1 86168 574 2

Printed in Great Britain
MWL Print Group Ltd

CONTENTS

Chapter 1 Child Labour

Child exploitation   1

Frequently asked questions about child labour   3

Facts on child labour 2010   6

The face of child labour from Africa to Asia and the Americas   9

Emerging economies 'worst for child labour risk'   11

Domestic labour   12

The consumer and child labour   13

ILO fears the goal of eliminating child labour by 2016 may not be reached   15

Chapter 2 Commercial Sexual Exploitation

The commercial sexual exploitation of children   16

Safeguarding children and young people from sexual exploitation   20

'They like us naïve': how teenage girls are groomed for a life of prostitution by UK gangs   24

Trafficked and exploited children   27

Fifth of Britons unknowingly aid child trafficking, according to survey   30

Concerns raised over low number of convictions for child trafficking   31

Chapter 3 Child Soldiers

Questions and answers about child soldiers   32

Fighting isn't just for boys: girls go to war   35

Rebuilding the lives of Congo's child soldiers   37

Key Facts   40

Glossary   41

Index   42

Acknowledgements   43

Assignments   44

OTHER TITLES IN THE ISSUES SERIES

For more on these titles, visit: www.independence.co.uk

Stress and Anxiety ISBN 978 1 86168 314 4
Customers and Consumerism ISBN 978 1 86168 386 1
A Genetically Modified Future? ISBN 978 1 86168 390 8
The Education Problem ISBN 978 1 86168 391 5
Vegetarian and Vegan Diets ISBN 978 1 86168 406 6
Media Issues ISBN 978 1 86168 408 0
The Cloning Debate ISBN 978 1 86168 410 3
Sustainability and Environment ISBN 978 1 86168 419 6
The Terrorism Problem ISBN 978 1 86168 420 2
Religious Beliefs ISBN 978 1 86168 421 9
A Classless Society? ISBN 978 1 86168 422 6
Migration and Population ISBN 978 1 86168 423 3
Climate Change ISBN 978 1 86168 424 0
Euthanasia and the Right to Die
ISBN 978 1 86168 439 4
Sexual Orientation and Society
ISBN 978 1 86168 440 0
The Gender Gap ISBN 978 1 86168 441 7
Domestic Abuse ISBN 978 1 86168 442 4
Travel and Tourism ISBN 978 1 86168 443 1
The Problem of Globalisation
ISBN 978 1 86168 444 8
The Internet Revolution ISBN 978 1 86168 451 6
An Ageing Population ISBN 978 1 86168 452 3
Poverty and Exclusion ISBN 978 1 86168 453 0
Waste Issues ISBN 978 1 86168 454 7
Staying Fit ISBN 978 1 86168 455 4
Drugs in the UK ISBN 978 1 86168 456 1
The AIDS Crisis ISBN 978 1 86168 468 4
Bullying Issues ISBN 978 1 86168 469 1
Marriage and Cohabitation ISBN 978 1 86168 470 7
Our Human Rights ISBN 978 1 86168 471 4
Privacy and Surveillance ISBN 978 1 86168 472 1
The Animal Rights Debate ISBN 978 1 86168 473 8
Body Image and Self-Esteem ISBN 978 1 86168 484 4
Abortion – Rights and Ethics ISBN 978 1 86168 485 1
Racial and Ethnic Discrimination ISBN 978 1 86168 486 8
Sexual Health ISBN 978 1 86168 487 5
Selling Sex ISBN 978 1 86168 488 2
Citizenship and Participation ISBN 978 1 86168 489 9
Health Issues for Young People ISBN 978 1 86168 500 1
Crime in the UK ISBN 978 1 86168 501 8
Reproductive Ethics ISBN 978 1 86168 502 5
Tackling Child Abuse ISBN 978 1 86168 503 2
Money and Finances ISBN 978 1 86168 504 9
The Housing Issue ISBN 978 1 86168 505 6
Teenage Conceptions ISBN 978 1 86168 523 0
Work and Employment ISBN 978 1 86168 524 7

Understanding Eating Disorders ISBN 978 1 86168 525 4
Student Matters ISBN 978 1 86168 526 1
Cannabis Use ISBN 978 1 86168 527 8
Health and the State ISBN 978 1 86168 528 5
Tobacco and Health ISBN 978 1 86168 539 1
The Homeless Population ISBN 978 1 86168 540 7
Coping with Depression ISBN 978 1 86168 541 4
The Changing Family ISBN 978 1 86168 542 1
Bereavement and Grief ISBN 978 1 86168 543 8
Endangered Species ISBN 978 1 86168 544 5
Responsible Drinking ISBN 978 1 86168 555 1
Alternative Medicine ISBN 978 1 86168 560 5
Censorship Issues ISBN 978 1 86168 558 2
Living with Disability ISBN 978 1 86168 557 5
Sport and Society ISBN 978 1 86168 559 9
Self-Harming and Suicide ISBN 978 1 86168 556 8
Sustainable Transport ISBN 978 1 86168 572 8
Mental Wellbeing ISBN 978 1 86168 573 5
Child Exploitation ISBN 978 1 86168 574 2
The Gambling Problem ISBN 978 1 86168 575 9
The Energy Crisis ISBN 978 1 86168 576 6
Nutrition and Diet ISBN 978 1 86168 577 3

A note on critical evaluation

Because the information reprinted here is from a number of different sources, readers should bear in mind the origin of the text and whether the source is likely to have a particular bias when presenting information (just as they would if undertaking their own research). It is hoped that, as you read about the many aspects of the issues explored in this book, you will critically evaluate the information presented. It is important that you decide whether you are being presented with facts or opinions. Does the writer give a biased or an unbiased report? If an opinion is being expressed, do you agree with the writer?

Child Exploitation offers a useful starting point for those who need convenient access to information about the many issues involved. However, it is only a starting point. Following each article is a URL to the relevant organisation's website, which you may wish to visit for further information.

Child exploitation

Information from Action on Child Exploitation.

What is child exploitation?

Child exploitation is a broad term which includes forced or dangerous labour, child trafficking and child prostitution. The term is used to refer to situations where children are abused – physically, verbally or sexually – or when they are submitted to unsatisfactory conditions as part of their forced or voluntary employment. Many of the children who suffer from exploitation do so because they have no other choice – their parents may need the added income, or the children may be orphaned or responsible for their siblings as a result of war or disease (particular HIV/AIDS). They may also have been trafficked or forced into slave labour, either in their own country or somewhere internationally, and may be living a life of struggle, suffering and invisibility within the community.

The International Labour Organization (ILO) believes that up to 1.2 million children are trafficked annually all over the world. The ILO defines human trafficking as the recruitment, transportation, transfer, harbouring and receipt of people (including children) by means of force, threat or coercion. Trafficking is only the beginning of the suffering for victims – generally those that are taken will be forced to work in industries that the ILO defines as some of the 'Worst Forms of Child Labour' (set out in the Worst Forms of Child Labour Convention). This includes prostitution; the drugs trade; and working dangerous jobs underground, underwater, in confined spaces, or in environments which can be harmful to the health.

> *Child exploitation is a broad term which includes forced or dangerous labour, child trafficking and child prostitution*

The ILO believes that no child should be submitted to these forms of employment, even if they are over the minimum work age decided upon by the country they work in. Unfortunately it is easy for governments to turn a blind eye to such child exploitation, and millions of children – 115 million at least – work in these 'Worst Forms' all over the world.

Where and why does it occur?

Child exploitation occurs all over the world, and for many different reasons. UNICEF believes that the overwhelming majority of countries have instances of (often unacknowledged) child exploitation – either through underage employment, or through more serious cases of abuse. The scary truth is that the UK has a serious problem with child exploitation – through the child sex trade and forced prostitution, and forced labour in homes, restaurants, factories and farms. These children are denied the right to attend school, may be separated from their families and friends and have no real hopes for the future. Although some of the more dangerous forms of child exploitation occur outside of the UK – in developing countries in Asia and Sub-Saharan Africa where labour is cheap and people do the jobs usually reserved for machines and factories – there is still a

significant problem within the UK which needs to be corrected. Unfortunately it was not until 2003 that the UK passed the Sexual Offences Act and 2004 that the Asylum and Immigration Act was passed. This shows clearly that the problem has only recently become more obvious to the wider community.

It is difficult for many people to understand why child exploitation occurs, and why it happens in successful, 'advanced' nations such as the UK. The majority of the reasons for exploitation are related to money – children provide cheap and obedient labour, and are small and can thus carry out difficult or unusual jobs. If the children are working to support their family they may be carrying out menial rural or industrial jobs which earn very little. If the children have been trafficked or are forced into labour against their will, they may not be paid at all – and their traffickers may be awarded fees for their use. Child exploitation is unfortunately big business, and this is one of the reasons why it continues into the 21st century.

The majority of the reasons for exploitation are related to money – children provide cheap and obedient labour, and are small and can thus carry out difficult or unusual jobs

How can it be stopped?

The fight against child exploitation is championed by several organisations, such as UNICEF, the ILO and the United Nations (UN). Over the last few decades all three have been striving to have the problem recognised by world governments, and they have also been pushing for legislation that should offer protection for children all over the globe.

In 1989 the UN put together the Convention on the Rights of the Child, which outlined the right of children to be protected from economic exploitation, and also the right to be protected from having to perform jobs that could be hazardous to their health or wellbeing. It also called for a minimum age of employment to be agreed and adhered to. The ILO supports the UN's policy, and has stated that they believe the minimum age of employment for children should be no younger than 15. This in effect should guarantee the child the right to a childhood, and potentially the right to an adequate education. In 2000 the UN followed up their Convention with the Protocol to Prevent, Suppress and Punish Trafficking in Persons, Especially Women and Children. This protocol became known as the Palermo Protocol, and was instigated to stem the tide of child exploitation. In 2003 UNICEF introduced the End Child Exploitation campaign which went on to 2005

and pressured the UK Government into agreeing to legislation that would guarantee a level of protection for child victims of trafficking, which was eventually agreed to in 2007. This was in place with the 2005 Council of Europe Convention on Trafficking in Human Beings, which the UK did not ratify until December 2008.

Sadly, although there is legislation in place that should force governments to be more stringent with monitoring and controls, child exploitation continues. The best way to get involved in the fight against child exploitation is by standing up and making yourself heard: lobby your local council, your government, and join organisations such as UNICEF.

⇨ The above information is reprinted with kind permission from Action on Child Exploitation. Visit www.ache.org.uk for more information.

© *Action on Child Exploitation*

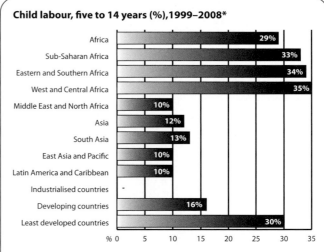

Child labour, five to 14 years (%),1999–2008*

	%
Africa	29%
Sub-Saharan Africa	33%
Eastern and Southern Africa	34%
West and Central Africa	35%
Middle East and North Africa	10%
Asia	12%
South Asia	13%
East Asia and Pacific	10%
Latin America and Caribbean	10%
Industrialised countries	-
Developing countries	16%
Least developed countries	30%

% 0   5   10   15   20   25   30   35

* *Data are for the most recent year available during the period specified.*

Source: The State of the World's Children, *November 2009, UNICEF (www.childinfo.org)*

Child labour, distribution by branch of economic activity (%), five to 17 years old

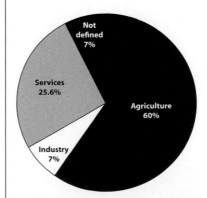

Not defined 7%

Services 25.6%

Agriculture 60%

Industry 7%

The agriculture sector comprises activities in agriculture; hunting; forestry, and fishing. The industry sector includes mining and quarrying; manufacturing; construction, and public utilities (electricity, gas and water). The services sector consists of wholesale and retail trade; restaurants and hotels; transport, storage, and communications; finance, insurance, real-estate, and business services; and community as well as social personal services.

Source: Global child labour developments: Measuring trends from 2004 to 2008, *Statistical Information and Monitoring Programme on Child Labour (SIMPOC), International Programme on the Elimination of Child Labour (IPEC), Copyright © 2010 International Labour Organization*

View full report at http://www.ilo.org/ipecinfo/product/download.do?type=document&id=13313. More information about child labour can be found on the IPEC website (www.ilo.org/ipec).

ACTION ON CHILD EXPLOITATION

Frequently asked questions about child labour

Information from Stop Child Labour.

What is 'child labour'?

'Stop Child Labour. School is the best place to work' fights child labour in all forms of work performed by children under the age of 14 that is detrimental to their physical and psychological health and development, and interferes with attending formal, full-time education. Child labour encompasses every non-school-going child irrespective of whether the child is engaged in wage or non-wage work. Child labour thus means all work that interferes with the right of the child to full-time, formal education and/or is hazardous. Small tasks, performed after school at home or at a farm, are thus not considered child labour.

There is, however, no universally accepted definition of 'child labour'. Writers and speakers don't always specify what definition they are using, and that often leads to confusion.

Definitions of 'child labour'

'Child labour' is, generally speaking, work for children, that harms them or exploits them in some way (physically, mentally, morally, or by blocking access to education).

But there is no universally accepted definition of 'child labour'. International organisations, non-governmental organisations, trade unions and other interest groups use varying definitions of the term.

For instance: international conventions adopted by the United Nations and the International Labour Organization define 'child' as anyone below the age of 18, and 'child labour' as some types of work performed by children below age 18. And yet ILO conventions variously define the appropriate minimum age of work as age 15 or under 14 in developing nations; while, in another convention, the definition of the 'worst' forms of work applies to all children under age 18. Governments, adding to the confusion, do not always use 18 as the cut-off point for defining a 'child'. International organisations such as UNICEF, and some social scientists, make a distinction between 'child work' (not objectionable) and 'child labour' (objectionable).

Not all work is bad for children. Some social scientists point out that some kinds of work may be completely unobjectionable. For instance, a child who delivers newspapers before school might actually benefit from learning how to work, gaining responsibility, and a bit of money. But what if the child is not paid? Then he or she is being exploited. As UNICEF's 1997 *State of the World's Children* report puts it, 'Children's work needs to be seen as happening along a continuum, with destructive or exploitative work at one end and beneficial work – promoting or enhancing children's development without interfering with their schooling, recreation and rest – at the other. And between these two poles are vast areas of work that need not negatively affect a child's development.' Other social scientists have slightly different ways of drawing the line between acceptable and unacceptable work.

International conventions also define 'child labour' as activities such as soldiering and prostitution. Not everyone agrees with this definition. Some child workers themselves think that illegal work (such as prostitution) should not be considered in the definition of 'child labour'. The reason: these child workers would like to be respected for their legal work, because they feel they have no other choice but to work. For further discussion of this dispute, see *New Internationalist* magazine, No. 292, July 1997 issue on Child Labour.

To avoid confusion, when writing or speaking about 'child labour', it's best to explain exactly what you mean by child labour – or, if someone else is speaking, ask for a definition. This article uses the first definition cited here: 'Child labour' is work for children under age 18 that in some way harms or exploits them (physically, mentally, morally, or by blocking children from education).

What is a child?

International conventions define children as aged 18 and under.

Individual governments may define 'child' differently, according to different ages or other criteria.

'Child' and 'childhood' are also defined differently in different cultures – and the definition is not necessarily delineated by age. Social scientists point out that children's abilities and maturities vary so much that defining a child's maturity by calendar age can be misleading. For a discussion, see Jo Boyden, Birgitta Ling, William Myers, *What Works for Working Children* (Stockholm: Radda Barnen and UNICEF, 1998), pp. 9-26.

How many 'child labourers' are there?

An estimated 200 million child workers between the ages of five and 14 work part-time and full-time, according to the ILO. But the ILO admits that this number does not include children – especially millions of girl children – who work at home and are not paid.

UNICEF's *State of the World's Children* report says only that, although the exact number is not known, it is surely in the hundreds of millions.

More information about who child labourers are, where they live, and new statistics on the total number can be found on the International Labour Organization's website at www.ilo.org

Do poor families need the extra income?

It appears in practice that child labour is generally not needed to help families survive. Child labourers usually contribute very little to the income and wellbeing of a family. Poverty does therefore not have to be an obstacle for attending regular daytime education.

'The poverty argument doesn't hold,' says Shantha Sinha, director of the MV Foundation in India. 'If you ask if extremely poor and desperate people send their children to work, then the answer is of course: yes. Generally, it is however not true that the poorest children are the first ones to drop out of school. There is a legion of schools in small villages where the poorest children do attend whereas their richer friends are at work.

'Arguments that are based on the "harsh reality" of poverty and the importance of a child's contribution to a family income are therefore hostile to a child and an impediment to their development.'

Naturally, it cannot be denied that the loss of income and additional costs of education can be a problem for a family at first. According to the MV Foundation, the families that do send their children to school are not becoming any poorer. Most parents are capable and willing to compensate for the lost income as soon as the school has proved to function adequately.

Moreover, it turns out that parents can demand a higher income from their employers when large groups of 'cheap' children are no longer available. Women especially – often with a lower income than men – can demand higher wages and better working hours when they no longer have to compete with their children on the labour market.

It can therefore be said that education is ultimately the only way to break out of the cycle of poverty.

Why is child labour hazardous?

Child labour deprives children of their childhood and future. It interferes with the child's right to rest and play and can, moreover, endanger the child's health. Many child labourers are so-called 'nowhere' children: they are neither enrolled in school nor registered as child labourers. They are therefore hardly visible to the outside world and fall outside the protective environment that a school can provide.

Without education children are, moreover, pre-destined to become illiterate labourers without an opportunity to develop their full potential. Child labour thus keeps the vicious cycle of poverty and ignorance in place.

Why is education so important?

Education is the key to poverty reduction and full citizenship. Quality education provides children with dignity, offers them a possibility to think, make choices and form their own opinion. Educated children have learned to defend themselves and claim their rights. Education is the foundation to a better life.

Moreover, education enhances sustainable development, the building of a democratic society and improves health conditions. The education of girls especially gives a high return in terms of improvement of health, family planning and the wellbeing of whole families. Also, women who have attended schools make extra efforts to ensure an education for their children as well.

The importance of basic education for all children is expressed in the combined mandate of the Convention on the Rights of the Child (CRC), the Child Labour Conventions 138 and 182 of the International Labour Organization (ILO) and the Millennium Development Goals (MDGs) aimed at the realisation of basic education for all children (boys and girls) by the year 2015. The international community thus agreed that education is a life skill and a basic right for all children.

How can child labour be eliminated?

The elimination of child labour is interlinked with the provision of full-time, formal and quality education free of charge to all. Many children do not have a choice but to work because there is no (well-functioning) educational system available or because they are not stimulated to attend education. During the Industrial Revolution it was possible to eliminate child labour in Europe due to a combined mandate of prohibiting child labour and implementing compulsory education. This should also happen in developing countries.

However, the discussion on 'Education for All' is often held without consideration of the fact that child labour is a huge obstacle for a large number of children to attend school. Building schools and improving the quality of education is therefore not enough. It is also essential to take a more active approach towards child labour (including child domestic labour) by developing specific strategies, to be able to mainstream all children under the age of 14 into schools.

Governments are responsible for the educational system and they should take up this responsibility. It is not only important that quality education is offered to children already in school. It is important that programmes for

STOP CHILD LABOUR

basic education in developing countries include a strategy that is mainstreaming working and other non-school-going children below the age of 14 into formal, full-time education.

Likewise, it is essential to establish a norm that work must never be an impediment for children to attend basic daytime education. As long as the community is accepting that children work instead of going to school, child labour and low school participation will not be eradicated.

Why do girls need special attention?

Two-thirds of all children that are not going to school are girls. The work that they perform is often hardly visible, e.g. in one's own or someone else's household (domestic child labour). This work is denying these girl children their right to education.

The backward position of girl children is a consequence of the belief that girls do not need to be educated because they will become housewives anyway. In some communities girl children drop out of school early because of child marriages. Moreover, girl children are often taken out of school because it is considered inappropriate and dangerous to walk long distances to school.

At the moment there is fortunately more attention for the arrears of girls in their participation in basic education. This should, however, be tied to an equal attention for the 'hidden' work of girls that is often the largest obstacle to their participation in full-time education.

What is the most important reason for children to work instead of attending schools?

Child labour is not just a matter of poverty. Apart from the income of the family, other factors play an important role in the decision of parents to send their children to school or to work. Experience from India shows that the exclusion of certain groups, existing social norms, tradition, parental ignorance, indifference from the Government and no education system (or a badly run education system) are the main determinants for parents not to send their children to school. According to Shantha Sinha, director of the MV Foundation, child labour exists in communities where:

⇨ there is no tradition of sending children to schools and little social pressure to do so;

⇨ existing social norms accept child labour, parents do not have an alternative and employers take advantage of the situation;

⇨ the educational system does not want to register and educate poor, lower-class children.

Isn't child labour normal in non-western cultures?

In western countries child labour used to be the norm too. The elimination of all forms of child labour in western countries succeeded because people made an effort to go against the ruling beliefs about child labour. Nowadays, these efforts are made by organisations like the MV Foundation in India. The MV Foundation is an Indian organisation with an Indian board and staff. They are fighting child labour and promoting education because they believe in what is best for India's children. It can therefore not be said that a western idea or belief is imposed on them.

An estimated 200 million child workers between the ages of five and 14 work part-time and full-time, according to the International Labour Organization

---

Almost all countries in the world, western and non-western, signed the Convention on the Rights of a Child (CRC). The elimination of child labour and the right to education is important for all children, wherever they were born.

What does 'School is the best place to work' want from the Government and the European Union?

'School is the best place to work' is calling on governments to:

1 Create a coherent policy on the elimination of child labour linked to the provision of full-time, formal education for all children up to 14 years of age.

2 Ensure that European Union members work together to allocate at least eight per cent of Overseas Development Aid to formal primary education, including strategies to integrate all out-of-school children into the education system.

3 Make provisions in Overseas Development aid to ensure that girls and young children from vulnerable groups (including those living in absolute poverty) are integrated into the formal school system.

⇨ The above information is reprinted with kind permission from Stop Child Labour. Visit www.stopchildlabour.net for more information.

© Stop Child Labour

STOP CHILD LABOUR

Facts on child labour 2010

Information from the International Labour Organization.

For over a decade, child labour has been recognised as a key issue of human rights at work, together with freedom of association, the right to collective bargaining, the abolition of forced labour, and non-discrimination in occupation and employment. However, despite the large social reform movement that has been generated around this issue, more than 200 million children worldwide are still in child labour and a staggering 115 million – at least – are subject to its worst forms.

The global campaign to end child labour is at a critical juncture. As the new Global Report under the follow-up to the ILO Declaration on Fundamental Principles and Rights at Work* shows, child labour continues to decline worldwide but at a much slower pace than before. The report, entitled *Accelerating action against child labour*, says there are clear signs of progress but also disconcerting gaps in the global response.

The new trends point to a major shift in the international fight against child labour compared to 2006. Then, encouraged by the positive results of the second Global Report, the ILO set the target of 2016 for eliminating the worst forms of child labour. Almost half-way towards that date, the report shows that in some critical parts of the world the fight is in danger of being lost. It warns that if current trends continue, the 2016 target will not be reached. There have been a number of leadership initiatives over the past years and important achievements in advocacy, enhanced partnerships, support of corporate social responsibility, data collection and research. Perhaps the most important step forward has been the overwhelming global consensus in support of the Education for All** movement. However, a renewed sense of commitment is needed. Governments have options when it comes to policy choices and budgetary allocations. The current global economic crisis cannot serve as an excuse to shift our priorities. A world free of child labour is possible.

* *Accelerating action against child labour*, Global Report under the follow-up to the ILO Declaration on fundamental Principles and Rights at Work. Report to the International Labour Conference, 99th Session 2010. ISBN: 978-92-2-121873-9.

** Education for All is a global movement aiming to meet the learning needs of all children, youth and adults by 2015.

Among the report's key findings

⇨ Child labour continues to decline, but only modestly – a three per cent reduction in the four-year period covered by the new estimates (2004-08). In the previous report (covering the period 2000-04), there had been a ten per cent decrease.

⇨ The global number of child labourers stands at 215 million, only seven million less than in 2004.

⇨ Among five- to 14-year-olds, the number of children in child labour has declined by ten per cent and the number of children in hazardous work by 31 per cent.

⇨ Whilst the number of children in hazardous work, often used as a proxy for the worst forms of child labour, is declining, the overall rate of reduction has slowed. There are still 115 million children in hazardous work.

⇨ There has been a welcome 15 per cent decrease in the number of girls in child labour and a 24 per cent decline in the number of girls in hazardous work. Boys, however, saw their work increase, both in terms of incidence rates and in absolute numbers. The extent of hazardous work among boys remained relatively stable.

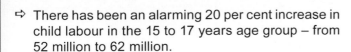

⇨ There has been an alarming 20 per cent increase in child labour in the 15 to 17 years age group – from 52 million to 62 million.

⇨ With regard to children aged five to 14 in economic activity, the Asian-Pacific region and Latin America and the Caribbean experienced a decrease. In contrast, for the same age group, the number of children in economic activity is increasing in Sub-Saharan Africa. The situation is particularly alarming in Sub-Saharan Africa, where one in four children aged five to 17 are child labourers, compared to one in eight in Asia-Pacific and one in ten in Latin America and the Caribbean.

⇨ Most child labourers continue to work in agriculture (60 per cent). Only one in five working children is in paid employment. The overwhelming majority are unpaid family workers.

⇨ There has been considerable progress in the ratification of ILO standards concerning child labour, namely of Conventions 182 (on the worst forms of child labour) and 138 (on minimum age). However, one-third of the children in the world live in countries that have not ratified these conventions.

Most child labourers continue to work in agriculture (60 per cent). Only one in five working children is in paid employment. The overwhelming majority are unpaid family workers

Global goals

Encouraged by the positive results of the second Global Report on Child Labour in 2006, the ILO set the deadline of eradicating the worst forms of child labour by 2016. The ILO's Global Action Plan is based on three pillars:

⇨ supporting and mainstreaming national responses to child labour;

⇨ deepening and strengthening the worldwide movement against child labour;

⇨ further integrating child labour concerns in overall ILO strategies to promote decent work for all.

The Global Action Plan urged countries to design and put in place appropriate time-bound measures by 2008. Judging from the results of the third Global Report, many, if not most, countries have failed to do so. What's more, in the broader context of progress on the Millennium Development Goals (MDGs), and in particular the pace regarding universal primary education, the signs are not too encouraging either.

Global action

The International Programme on the Elimination of Child Labour (IPEC) was created in 1992 to enhance the ILO's response to its long-standing goal of the effective elimination of child labour. Since then, IPEC has grown to become the biggest dedicated child labour programme in the world and the largest technical cooperation programme within the ILO with over $60 million expenditure in 2008.

Some other facts about IPEC:

⇨ By 2009, IPEC was operational in 92 countries in all regions of the world.

⇨ During the biennium 2008-09, IPEC activities benefited some 300,000 children directly and over 52 million indirectly.

In 2008, IPEC set out its vision for the next five years:

⇨ consolidate its position as the leading centre of knowledge and expertise on action against child labour;

⇨ maintain and further strengthen its research and data collection capacity, which form the basis for both targeted interventions and policy advice;

⇨ continue to be the central technical cooperation programme for action against child labour;

⇨ facilitate country-to-country technical cooperation within regions and across continents;

⇨ strengthen the worldwide movement against child labour and assume for the ILO a leadership role in the movement;

⇨ continue the integration of IPEC activities within ILO programming, most importantly within Decent Work Country Programmes.

The fight against child labour – timeline

Eliminating child labour is an essential element in the ILO's goal of 'Decent Work for All'. The ILO tackles child labour not as an isolated issue but as an integral part of national efforts for economic and social development.

1919 The first International Labour Conference adopts the first international Convention against child labour, the Minimum Age (Industry) Convention (No. 5).

1930 Adoption of the first Forced Labour Convention (No. 29).

1973 Adoption of the Minimum Age Convention (No. 138).

1992 The ILO establishes the International Programme on the Elimination of Child Labour (IPEC).

INTERNATIONAL LABOUR ORGANIZATION

1997 Amsterdam and Oslo International Conferences. These events helped raise international awareness of the child labour problem and the need for a forward-looking strategy.

1998 Adoption of the ILO Declaration on Fundamental Principles and Rights at Work: freedom of association, abolition of forced labour, end of discrimination in the workplace and elimination of child labour. All ILO member States pledge to uphold and promote these principles.

1999 Adoption of the ILO's Worst Forms of Child Labour Convention (No. 182). Focused world attention on the need to take immediate action to eradicate those forms of child labour that are hazardous and damaging to children's physical, mental or moral wellbeing. Ratified by nine out of ten of the ILO's member States.

2002 The ILO publishes its first Global Report on child labour and establishes 12 June as World Day Against Child Labour. The Organization supports more than 80 countries in formulating their own programmes to combat child labour.

2004 First ILO global study on the costs and benefits of eliminating child labour says that benefits would outweigh costs by nearly six to one.

2006 Encouraged by findings of the second global report on child labour, which says that child labour is declining worldwide, the ILO launches a global campaign to eliminate the worst forms of child labour by 2016.

2008 The ILO adopts the ILO Declaration on Social Justice for a Fair Globalization, which recognises the particular significance of the fundamental rights, including the effective abolition of child labour.

2009 The 183 member States of the ILO unanimously adopt the Global Jobs Pact as a guide to recovery from the global economic and jobs crisis. The Pact calls for increased vigilance to achieve the elimination and prevention of an increase of forced labour, child labour and discrimination at work.

2010 The ILO launches the third Global Report on child labour, warning that the pace and profile of progress is not fast enough to achieve the 2016 deadline of eliminating the worst forms of child labour worldwide.

2010 The Hague Global Child Labour Conference aimed at strengthening progress towards the 2016 target and the ratification and implementation of Conventions 138 and 182. For more information on the ILO's International Programme on the Elimination of Child Labour (IPEC), please visit www.ilo.org/ipec

April 2010

⇨ The above information is reprinted with kind permission from the ILO International Programme on Child Labour (IPEC). Visit www.ilo.org/ipec for more. A catalogue containing details of further child domestic labour information resources can be downloaded from http://www.ilo.org/ipecinfo/product/viewProduct.do?productId=3924

Copyright © 2010 International Labour Organization

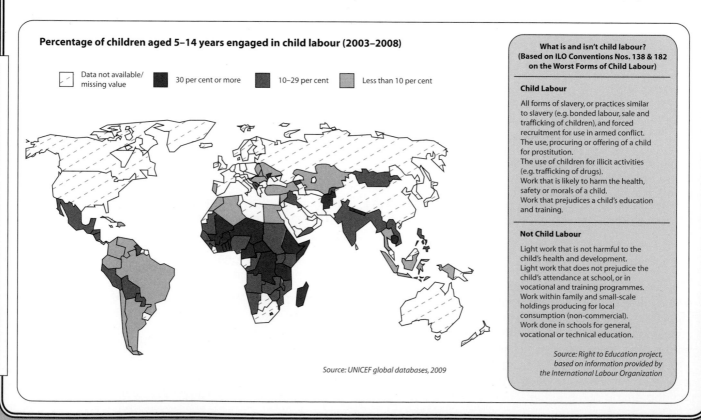

Percentage of children aged 5–14 years engaged in child labour (2003–2008)

Data not available/missing value — 30 per cent or more — 10–29 per cent — Less than 10 per cent

Source: UNICEF global databases, 2009

What is and isn't child labour?
(Based on ILO Conventions Nos. 138 & 182 on the Worst Forms of Child Labour)

Child Labour

All forms of slavery, or practices similar to slavery (e.g. bonded labour, sale and trafficking of children), and forced recruitment for use in armed conflict.
The use, procuring or offering of a child for prostitution.
The use of children for illicit activities (e.g. trafficking of drugs).
Work that is likely to harm the health, safety or morals of a child.
Work that prejudices a child's education and training.

Not Child Labour

Light work that is not harmful to the child's health and development.
Light work that does not prejudice the child's attendance at school, or in vocational and training programmes.
Work within family and small-scale holdings producing for local consumption (non-commercial).
Work done in schools for general, vocational or technical education.

Source: Right to Education project, based on information provided by the International Labour Organization

INTERNATIONAL LABOUR ORGANIZATION

The face of child labour from Africa to Asia and the Americas

Some important progress has been made in tackling child labour but it's still here and has the power to haunt. Globally, there are now 30 million fewer working children than ten years ago. However, there are still an estimated 215 million girls and boys trapped in child labour.

In 2006, the pace of progress was such that the international community set an ambitious goal: to eliminate the worst forms of child labour within ten years. But in more recent years progress toward this goal has slowed. And many of the children now remaining in child labour are among the hardest to reach.

Between March and May 2010, Elaine Moore, a Phnom Penh-based journalist, and ILO photographer Marcel Crozet, visited three countries on three continents. The examples that follow show that there can be progress when there is determined action to tackle child labour. However, there is a need to scale up such actions. The key to this is renewing and strengthening political commitment and developing integrated policies and programmes to fight child labour.

Child labour in Cambodia: a new direction

Although Cambodia is emerging as one of the brightest economic growth stories of South-East Asia, over 313,000 children are trapped in the worst forms of exploitation such as drug trafficking and prostitution. But the end of all worst forms of child labour in the country could be within reach, and the Cambodian Government has committed itself to taking on the challenge, as have the social partners. But in order to stay the course it will require the continued support of those inside the country, as well as a continued financial commitment from donors, to ensure that every child in Cambodia is given the start in life they deserve.

On a hot afternoon in Cambodia's capital city Phnom Penh, ten-year-old Leap beckons to tourists riding by on the back of a lumbering elephant. Struggling to carry her basket of snacks she runs along a dusty road next to the golden Royal Palace offering rice cakes and sweets from a container too big for her small arms.

Leap has already been working for five hours and, most likely, will still be out here at midnight. Working alone, Leap is a small vulnerable girl who has never been to school and who will be lucky if she earns two dollars today. Leap says she has no choice. If she were to stop working, her mother and younger brothers would go hungry.

In another part of the city, seven-year-old Doung Paeaktra crouches down near a riverbank sifting through a pile of rubbish. He's looking for plastic he can sell to a recycler. With his father dead and his mother at home nursing a new baby, Doung is the sole provider for his family.

Access to education has improved in Cambodia but child labour persists – Leap and Doung are two of the children still left behind. While primary school enrolment has risen from 75 per cent in 1997 to 91 per cent in 2005, most of the children attending school are combining their studies with work.

One of the ILO's responses has been to pioneer a livelihood scheme to help decrease, and eventually eliminate, a family's reliance on its children for income. This IPEC programme encourages parents and other adults from the country's poorest families to work together to create savings groups.

In a small village in southern Cambodia, local women explain how their savings group has helped them set up small businesses and supplemented that with training in finance and administration. 'Before the group, things were very difficult and the children had to work,' says 60-year-old Pan Phen. 'If I had problems I would have to go to the moneylender who charges 20 per cent interest monthly. Now I make more money and in our group the interest rate is just three per cent.' Pan Phen borrowed 40,000 riel (US$10) from the group and now makes sweets which she sells outside a local factory each day. 'All (six) of the children I look after are now in school,' she adds proudly.

In many cases, families of child labourers want to send their children to school but they find it hard to survive when the money the child earns stops, especially if there is an emergency at home such as a new baby or a death in the family.

Eliminating child labour in Bolivia: the role of education

Education is often cited as the key to eliminating child labour. But by itself, education isn't enough. The following report from Bolivia shows how adding decent work for adults to education of children, together with a quotient of political will, can make the equation work.

INTERNATIONAL LABOUR ORGANIZATION

When 11-year-old Juanita Avillo Ari and her six brothers and sisters arrived at the foot of a mine in this southern Bolivian city seven years ago, she and her family were in dire straits.

Juanita and her family had exhausted the capacity of their small plot of agricultural land in a rural community to feed them, let alone make a living. Like hundreds of other families, they wound up at a mine at the Cerro Rico mountain, where her father found work as a miner and her mother as a guard. The long working hours meant that Juanita and her siblings were often left alone in a precarious hut at the camp. When her older brothers left to start families of their own, life for Juanita and her two other siblings became lonelier and even more precarious. They would have suffered the same fate as many other children in the mining camps, who are exposed to hazardous child labour navigating narrow tunnels, if her parents hadn't been approached by the CEPROMIN (Centro de Promoción Minera) non-governmental organisation.

CEPROMIN runs a project on improving the living conditions of children and mining families living in the mining camps of Potosí. Juanita and her brothers are among some 450 children now enrolled in the project.

The project makes sure they are properly fed and looked after and, most importantly, that they receive a quality education. In addition, the project addresses the needs of adults, improving the socio-economic environment. This combined approach can make a big difference.

Juanita had never attended school but since joining the project she has proven to be one of the smartest students in the class. She dreams of continuing her studies and of a better life. However, Juanita is one of the fortunate children.

Fixing the future of Mali's child workers

In Mali, approximately two out of three children aged five to 17 work. This represents over three million children. Few of them go to school and 40 per cent of children aged five to 14 perform hazardous tasks. The situation of migrant girls is of particular concern.

'When I met Mouna for the first time I could hardly believe that she was only nine years old… if her frail body was indeed the one of a girl, her face already looked like the one of an old woman,' says ILO photographer Marcel Crozet. From 7am to 8pm Mouna works as a maid for a family in the village of Douentza.

For 2,000 francs CFA (3.05 euros) per month, she takes care of the children, prepares the meals, draws heavy buckets of water from a well, washes the dishes and cleans the house. Tonight she has come to seek help at a centre run by the NGO AVES (Avenir Enfance Sahel) because she has not been paid for four months and is not able to eat every day… A representative of the NGO will accompany her tomorrow to meet and discuss the matter with the family that employs her. This kind of intervention is usually very effective.

The next day at six o'clock in the morning, during a visit to a 'landlady', we meet 15-year-old Awa, another domestic worker. In a windowless room of 12 square metres the landlady houses 15 young girls from the same village she used to live in. They sleep on mats on the floor and all their belongings fit into a plastic bag.

Awa is alone – the other girls have already left for work. For three days, she had suffered from a severe attack of malaria. It is time for the doctor employed by AVES to intervene with the appropriate treatment...

AVES, one of the ILO's partner organisations in Mali, aims at curbing the rural exodus of girls and at protecting them from dangers, including sexual exploitation.

Its activities include education, health promotion, vocational training and support for income-generating activities. ILO-IPEC is working closely with government, employers' and workers' organisations to identify ways of scaling up such programmes.

In Mali, more than 50,000 children, over 35,000 of whom are girls, have benefited from ILO action programmes. Free schooling systems have been put in place for children working in agricultural areas, thereby removing them from a dangerous work environment without adding an unbearable financial burden to their parents.

August 2010

⇨ The above information is reprinted with kind permission from the ILO International Programme on Child Labour (IPEC). Visit www.ilo.org/ipec for more. A catalogue containing details of further child domestic labour information resources can be downloaded from http://www.ilo.org/ipecinfo/product/viewProduct.do?productId=3924

Emerging economies 'worst for child labour risk'

Information from the Institute of Risk Management.

By Graham Buck

The emerging economies of Bangladesh, China, India, Nigeria and Pakistan are rated as the countries with most risk of human rights violations against underage workers in a new survey.

The Child Labour Index, which rates 196 countries on the use of child workers within their labour markets, has important ethical implications for companies needing to manage risk within supply chains reaching across these countries.

The index and map, produced by global risks advisory firm Maplecroft, rates 68 countries as 'extreme risk' of widespread abuse of child labour. Many of 'the key emerging economies that supply the world with manufactured goods and natural resources, and that are fuelling the global economic recovery, have the worst record of underage workers within their labour markets,' it notes.

Both India and China recently featured in damaging revelations for an international fashion chain, where suppliers used by the company were found to be employing children for less than the minimum wage

The index evaluates the prevalence, gravity and impunity of child labour under the age of 15 that is defined as work that directly or indirectly limits or damages a child's physical, mental, social or psychological development.

Bangladesh, India, Nigeria and Pakistan all scored 0.00 out of a possible ten, along with Chad, DR Congo, Ethiopia, Liberia, Myanmar, Somalia, Sudan and Zimbabwe to form the 12 countries at the bottom of the ranking, whilst China scored 0.02 and ranked 13th.

Both India and China recently featured in damaging revelations for an international fashion chain, where suppliers used by the company were found to be employing children for less than the minimum wage; however, it is the rural sector where 70% of child labour is found.

'These large emerging economies are essential to the strategic interests of multinational business as they constitute a primary source for raw materials and manufactured goods,' said Monique Bianchi, principal analyst at Maplecroft. 'Not only is child labour wrong, but the existence of child labour within a company's value chain can have significant impacts on reputation and profits and it is critical that companies undertake stringent monitoring of all suppliers.'

India, ranked joint first in the index, is crucial not only to the textile sector, but also to the mining and ICT industries, amongst others. According to the latest government figures, India is home to between 14 million to 16.4 million child workers. However, these estimates are widely disputed and the US State Department puts the figure closer to 55 million. Child labour is most prominent in rural areas, particularly in the agricultural sector.

It is the rural sector where 70% of child labour is found

China now features in the supply chains of most multinational companies and Maplecroft advises businesses to be aware that child labour is prevalent throughout the country. Although there are no official statistics on the use of child labour in China, as the Government classifies such statistics as 'state secrets', it is thought there are between 10 million and 20 million underage workers. According to Maplecroft, companies working with suppliers in the textile, electronics and manufacturing sectors are particularly vulnerable to the risk of complicity with labour rights violations.

Vulnerability to the impacts of climate change will also contribute to increasing rates of child labour, suggests Maplecroft's chief executive Professor Alyson Warhurst: 'Drought and deforestation result in more work for children, as they must travel greater distances to gather water and fuel for farming purposes; whilst more frequent and severe climate-related disasters will lead to raised levels of poverty, forcing children from education and into the workforce to support their families.'

1 December 2010

⇨ The above information is reprinted with kind permission from the Institute of Risk Management. Visit www.theirm.org for more information.

© Institute of Risk Management

INSTITUTE OF RISK MANAGEMENT

Domestic labour

Global facts and figures in brief.

Throughout the world, thousands of children are working as domestic helpers, performing tasks such as cleaning, ironing, cooking, minding children and gardening. In many countries this phenomenon is not only socially and culturally accepted but might be regarded positively as a protected and non-stigmatised type of work, and therefore preferable to other forms of work, especially for the girl-child. The perpetuation of traditional female roles and responsibilities within and outside the household, and the perception of domestic service as part of a woman's apprenticeship for adulthood and marriage, also contribute to the low recognition of domestic work as a form of economic activity, and of child domestic labour as a form of child labour.

Ignorance of, or disregard for, the risks children might be exposed to in this kind of work is an alarming reality in many parts of the world. It is also one of the reasons for the widespread institutional reluctance to address the issue with specific policies and laws and why the issue has only recently come to the forefront of the international debate as potentially one of the most widespread 'worst forms of child labour'.

Given its hidden nature, it is impossible to have reliable figures on how many children are globally exploited as domestic workers. According to the ILO, though, more girl-children under 16 are in domestic service than in any other category of child labour. Available statistics mostly based on local research and surveys, and certainly only the tip of the iceberg, provide for an alarming indication of the extent of the phenomenon worldwide. Recent IPEC rapid assessments conducted in Asia, Africa and Latin America confirm the overwhelming extent and gravity of this problem.

According to recent reports, for example, some 175,000 children under 18 are employed in domestic service in Central America, more than 688,000 in Indonesia alone, 53,942 under 15 in South Africa and 38,000 children between five and seven in Guatemala.

The root causes of child domestic labour are multiple and multi-faceted. Poverty and its feminisation, social exclusion, lack of education, gender and ethnic discrimination, domestic violence, displacement, rural-urban migration and loss of parents due to conflicts and diseases are just some of the multiple 'push factors' for child domestic workers worldwide. Increasing social and economic disparities, debt bondage, the perception that the employer is simply an extended 'family' and protected environment for the child, the increasing need for the women of the household to have a 'replacement' at home that will enable more and more of them to enter the labour market, and the illusion that domestic service gives the child worker an opportunity for education, are some of its 'pull factors'.

The hazards linked to this practice are a matter of serious concern. The ILO has identified a number of hazards to which domestic workers are particularly vulnerable and the reason it may be considered to be one of the worst forms of child labour. Some of the most common risks children face in domestic service are:

⇨ long and tiring working days;

⇨ use of toxic chemicals;

⇨ carrying heavy loads;

⇨ handling dangerous items, such as knives, axes and hot pans;

⇨ insufficient or inadequate food and accommodation,;

⇨ humiliating or degrading treatment, including physical and verbal violence, and sexual abuse.

Thousands of children are working as domestic helpers

These hazards need to be seen in association with the denial of fundamental rights of the children such as, for example, access to education and health care, the right to rest, leisure, play and recreation and the right to be cared for and to have regular contact with their parents and peers (UN Convention on the Rights of the Child). These factors can have an irreversible physical, psychological and moral impact on the development, health and wellbeing of the child.

Given the complexity of its root causes and impact, any effort to adequately and efficiently address child domestic labour must therefore be of a multidisciplinary, multi-faceted and integrated nature, and linked to the broader context of poverty reduction, elimination and prevention of the worst forms of child labour and promotion and enforcement of fundamental labour and human rights.

⇨ The above information is reprinted with kind permission from the ILO International Programme on Child Labour (IPEC). Visit www.ilo.org/ipec for more. A catalogue containing details of further child domestic labour information resources can be downloaded from http://www.ilo.org/ipecinfo/product/viewProduct.do?productId=3924

Copyright © 2010 International Labour Organization

INTERNATIONAL LABOUR ORGANIZATION

The consumer and child labour

Information from Stop Child Labour.

Introduction

> 'Before you finish eating your breakfast this morning you've depended on half the world.'
>
> Martin Luther King Jr. (1929-68)

As consumers, we have power. We can make decisions about what we buy and who we buy from and in doing this we send a strong signal about the world we want to live in. A signal that retailers, manufacturers and businesses cannot ignore. With information, it is possible to make ethical consumer decisions. Ethical consumption can be about a range of issues including fair trade, respect for labour standards, environmental sustainability, animal welfare, community development and healthy eating. Consumers can demand that everything in our shopping baskets, on shelves and on clothes hangers has been produced without exploiting the planet and without exploiting people.

> 'Ethical shopping – and ethical consumerism in general – is about taking responsibility for your day-to-day impact on the world. It doesn't mean deluding yourself that shopping can solve all the world's problems, or that the checkout is the new ballot box. And it doesn't mean following a prescriptive list of evil companies and countries that need to be boycotted. It means taking the time to learn a little about how your lifestyle affects people, the planet and animals, and making your own decisions about what constitutes an ethical or unethical purchase.' Clark D., 2004, *The Rough Guide to Ethical Shopping*: vii

Ethical consuming is about buying things that are made ethically by companies that act ethically. Consumers everywhere can also 'look behind the label' of everything they buy to ensure that no child labour was used. This way, consumers make it clear to retailers that they must ensure that no child labour is used anywhere in the manufacture of the products they are selling.

Should we boycott?

Boycotts are not helpful given that they often hurt the people that they are trying to help. They could even make matters worse. For example, children could be forced from unsafe factories to even more unsafe streets.

Furthermore, child labour is so widespread and supply chains are so difficult to follow, it is hard to promote one company's record over another. Instead of refusing to buy certain products, consumers should use their power to support those organisations and initiatives that are creating the conditions for a child-labour-free world.

Brand manufacturers are very sensitive to consumer pressure, so we can put pressure on them to guarantee that no child labour was used in the making of their products. Such pressure can range from asking questions, writing letters directly to the company, retailers, business groups, chambers of commerce and politicians. We can also create demand for transparency and accountability in all supply chains.

Instead of refusing to buy certain products, consumers should use their power to support those organisations and initiatives that are creating the conditions for a child-labour-free world

---

Child labour will only be eliminated when systems are put in place to prevent one group of child labourers being replaced by another. We believe that child labour is not just an issue for a single industry or company alone, but an issue for all of us. We should all work together towards the elimination of child labour.

No one action will eliminate child labour. Instead, political mobilisation and public action is needed and to be successful, all stakeholders must be involved.

> 'Boycotts are something that may make the person who's boycotting feel better, but it doesn't necessarily make conditions any better for the child.' Carol Bellamy (former Executive Director of UNICEF) Campaign Resource

Focus on cotton

Cotton is one of the most traded agricultural raw materials in the world today and child labour is widespread in the cotton-producing industry. According to the Environmental Justice Foundation, six of the world's seven cotton producers have reportedly used children in their fields.

Children are involved in harvesting, producing hybrid seeds, applying pesticides and pest control. They are exposed to hazardous and dangerous conditions and hard, difficult labour – all at the expense of their

education. A global demand for cheap cotton is forcing children out of the classroom and into the cotton field.

'The link between children in fields and consumers in the west cannot be avoided.'

The Environmental Justice Foundation (EJF)

Some cotton facts

⇨ There are four main types of cotton: genetically modified, conventional, fair-trade and organic.

⇨ European and North American consumers account for 75% of world clothing imports. Therefore, these consumers can influence how the cotton industry operates.

⇨ 99% of cotton farmers live and work in the developing world where 70% of the world's cotton supply is produced. Two-thirds of these farmers live in India and China.

⇨ Cotton uses more insecticide than any other crop.

⇨ Child labour subsidises the cotton industry through free and cheap labour and the bargaining power of adults is greatly reduced.

⇨ One-third of textiles coming into the EU come from China, followed by Turkey and India. The UK and Germany are the biggest EU cotton importers.

⇨ 60% of the world's cotton is used for clothing, 35% is used in home furnishings and 5% is used in industrial products.

⇨ Subsidies to farmers in rich countries drive the price of cotton downwards. For example, the US cotton industry was subsidised by $4.2 billion in 2004/05. Sub-Saharan Africa lost $350 million as a result of reduced artificial world prices.

⇨ It is estimated that the removal of cotton subsidies would see an increase in household income by 2.3-5.7%. This would significantly increase family income, allowing farmers to, among other things, send their children to school.

Cotton and education

Cases of children missing out on their right to education can be found all over the world. For example, in Uzbekistan, state-imposed quotas force children out of the classroom and into the cotton fields. In central Asia, students are removed from school during harvest season and children are sent to work in cotton fields under the guise of 'summer camps'. In China, schools in the cotton-producing region are forced to undertake 'work-study' programmes, are under-funded and teachers are not paid. Poor-quality education sees a high drop-out rate and an

increase in the number of children working to supply the cotton industry. Children also migrate across borders during harvest season, missing out on their education for most of the school year.

Take action

'Consumers are fuelling a false economy that deprives children of their childhood and developing countries of an educated future generation.'

EJF

It is entirely possible and feasible to establish the source of all cotton. However, the cotton-producing industry will only take responsibility when it is pressurised to do so through political will and consumer action. Consumers must create demand for ethically- and sustainably-produced cotton.

Without labelling and completely transparent supply chains, the cotton industry is denying consumers the option to make informed choices about their purchases. Labels must indicate both the country of origin plus the country of manufacture. Consumers must demand to know who is handling cotton at every stage of its production.

For more information visit: www.continentalclothing.com and www.ejfoundation.org

⇨ Information from Stop Child Labour. Visit www.stopchildlabour.net for more.

© Stop Child Labour

STOP CHILD LABOUR

ILO fears the goal of eliminating child labour by 2016 may not be reached

Information from the Ghana News Agency.

Though a global report shows a modest decline in the rate of child labour, the International Labour Organization (ILO) has expressed doubt as to whether the goal of eliminating the menace by 2016 could be realised.

The Organization's 2008 Comprehensive Report puts the figure of children engaged in labour worldwide at 215 million, with 115 million of the number engaged in hazardous work. Mr Francesco d'Ovidio, Chief Technical Advisor of the International Programme on the Elimination of Child Labour (IPEC), made this known at the weekend during the media launch of the 2010 World Day Against Child Labour, held in Accra.

The event, under the theme 'Ghana Go for the Goal: End Child Labour', also saw the launch of the current ILO Child Labour Global Report. Mr d'Ovidio said there still existed strong factors that militated against the attainment of the international goal of eliminating the worst forms of child labour and therefore suggested measures to deal with the situation.

The implementation of national plans to tackle child labour; inclusion of child labour outcomes in national development plans; quality education; social protection of poor families, and law enforcement and child protection were some of his suggestions.

Others were: increasing international co-operation; strengthening co-operation with social partners; advocacy and mobilisation using communication tools, and decent work opportunities for adults. Mr Kabral Blay-Amihere, Chairman of the National Media Commission, urged journalists to serve as agents of change in their reportage to clamp down on child labour and its associated repercussions. He said they needed to investigate stories, do interviews and monitor events in order to make continuous and consistent inputs on issues bordering on child labour to achieve the needed impact. 'You need to set the agenda for the society. I appeal to you to feel the anguish of the African child and allow it to guide you to do a continuous report on the subject to effect a positive change in society,' he said.

Alluding to some legends of change, he said Bob Marley, a reggae pop star, sang on the themes of liberation and justice, adding they were qualities that were badly needed in some countries, including Zimbabwe. 'He sang about justice and liberation in Zimbabwe when others sang about love. His influence had been so remarkable that people continue to talk about him even though he is now dead,' he said. 'You have the chance of impacting the lives of children and it is up to you to do things differently in a positive way. It is a work that will not give you economic benefits now, but that which will give you recognition for the good work you do for society.'

Miss Anna Bossman, Deputy Commissioner for the Commission for Human Rights and Administrative Justice (CHRAJ), decried the prevalence of child labour in the country and called on the media to join in the fight against its worst forms.

Mr Ransford Tetteh, President of the Ghana Journalists Association, espoused the role of the media in tackling the issue of child labour, stressing that a clear and unambiguous way of communicating to the public was critical to eliminating the menace. He referred to child labour as not only being a social issue but an economic, legal, political and cultural one as well, adding that journalists needed to be properly acquainted with the issue to make meaningful and positive contributions.

Madam Stella Ofori, Principal Labour Officer at the Child Labour Unit of the Labour Department, said government had, through the Ministry of Employment and Social Welfare and with support from the ILO/IPEC, developed the National Plan of Actions (NPA) to eliminate worst forms of child labour. She said nine worst forms of child labour had been identified in the NPA as priority areas needing attention.

Madam Ofori said the areas included child trafficking, fisheries, mining and quarrying, ritual servitude, commercial sexual exploitation, child domestic servitude, portage of heavy loads, agriculture, street hawking and begging.

NPA is a comprehensive framework which seeks to promote a more co-ordinated effort towards the elimination of the worst forms of child labour. Its main objective is to reduce the worst forms of child labour to the barest minimum by 2015, while laying strong social, policy and institutional foundations for the elimination and prevention of all other forms of child labour in the longer term.

5 June 2010

⇨ The above information is reprinted with kind permission from the Ghana News Agency. Visit www. ghananewsagency.org for more information.

© Ghana News Agency

GHANA NEWS AGENCY

Chapter 2

COMMERCIAL SEXUAL EXPLOITATION

The commercial sexual exploitation of children

Questions and answers.

Who is a child?

Article 1 of the United Nations Convention on the Rights of the Child states that a child is a person below the age of 18, unless the age of majority is attained earlier under the national law applicable to the child. As such, 18 has become the age for determining childhood among the international child rights NGO community. However, there are states in which children are considered adults before 18 years of age or where protection measures do not apply through to 18. Different laws may provide for different ages of majority with significant variations within and across jurisdictions. When a state establishes a low age of majority – 14 for example – one of the most direct consequences is that those persons between 14 and 18 are likely excluded from the scope of the CRC because they will not be considered as 'children'. Where ages other than 18 are used to define a child, protection of children from sexual exploitation and related forms of violence becomes more difficult. This is especially true when children cross international borders and may not be subject to the equivalent levels of protection between states.

The age of sexual consent refers to the time at which a person is considered legally able to engage in sexual activity. The age of consent varies from country to country – and even within a country. It may also differ between genders, typically higher for males than for females, where legislation does not guarantee equal rights to men and women. Conversely, many of the laws which some countries have to protect children from sexual exploitation only address the issue in relation to girls' exploitation, whilst the sexual exploitation of boys is generally ignored. While there is no international consensus on what constitutes an appropriate age of sexual consent (it currently varies from 12 to 18), low ages of sexual consent increase children's vulnerability to commercial sexual exploitation of children (CSEC). In countries where the age of sexual consent is low, children who have reached that age are particularly vulnerable to abuse and exploitation, especially when there are no legal provisions that define and prohibit child sexual exploitation in prostitution and pornography. Children can never consent to being exploited and abused. It is therefore important that countries with low ages of sexual consent amend their laws to raise that age, and that laws

on sexual exploitation of children protect all children up to the age of 18, irrespective of the age of sexual consent.

The legal definition of a child also affects how offenders are dealt with by the courts. In some instances, social acceptance may affect the attitudes and approach of law enforcement and judicial officers with the result that abuses are considered 'less serious' and little action is taken.

> *Child sex tourism is the commercial sexual exploitation of children by people who travel from one location to another and there engage in sexual acts with minors*

What is commercial sexual exploitation of children?

Commercial sexual exploitation of children consists of criminal practices that demean and threaten the physical and psychosocial integrity of children. The Declaration and Agenda for Action against Commercial Sexual Exploitation of Children is a groundbreaking instrument that defines the commercial sexual exploitation of children as:

'A fundamental violation of children's rights. It comprises sexual abuse by the adult and remuneration in cash or kind to the child or a third person or persons. The child is treated as a sexual object and as a commercial object. The commercial sexual exploitation of children constitutes a form of coercion and violence against children, and amounts to forced labour and a contemporary form of slavery.'

The primary, interrelated forms of CSEC are prostitution of children, child pornography and trafficking of children for sexual purposes. Other forms include child sex tourism, and in some cases, child marriage. Children can also be commercially sexually exploited in other, less obvious ways, such as through domestic servitude or bonded labour. In these cases, a child is contracted to provide work but the employer believes that the child can also be used for sexual purposes.

Commercial sexual exploitation of children exists because there is a demand for it. Deterrence and criminal punishments are important, but any efforts to

end the commercial sexual exploitation of children must also recognise the need to challenge and condemn behaviours, beliefs and attitudes that support and sustain this demand.

It is important to note that not only girls, but also large numbers of boys, are exploited in commercial sex.

Prostitution of children

The Optional Protocol on the sale of children, child prostitution and child pornography (Optional Protocol) defines child prostitution as 'the use of a child in sexual activities for remuneration or any other form of consideration'. The prostitution of children thus occurs when someone benefits from a commercial transaction in which a child is made available for sexual purposes. Children may be controlled by an intermediary who manages or oversees the transaction, or by a sex exploiter, who negotiates directly with the child. Children are also involved in prostitution when they engage in sex in return for basic needs such as food, shelter or safety, or for favours such as higher grades at school or extra pocket money to purchase consumer goods. These acts may occur in many different locations, such as brothels, bars, clubs, homes, hotels or on the street.

The key issue is not that children make a choice to engage in prostitution in order to survive or to buy more consumer goods: driven by circumstances, or influenced by acquaintances, peers as well as social norms and values, they are pushed into situations in which adults take advantage of their vulnerability and sexually exploit and abuse them. In this sense, the terms 'child prostitute' or 'child sex worker' do not reflect the actual reality as they imply that a child has somehow chosen to make prostitution a profession. It is adults who create 'child prostitution' through their demand for children as sexual objects, their misuse of power and their desire for profit; as such, children are victims of abuse rather than 'sex workers'.

Commercial sexual exploitation of children through prostitution is a global problem and is closely connected to child pornography and the trafficking of children for sexual purposes. Demand for sex with children may come from both local and foreign exploiters. Local demand – which generally comprises persons who are perpetrators of commercial sexual exploitation of children in their country of origin – is a significant factor that is often overlooked. Almost universally, local demand for sex with children outnumbers the demand of foreigners in any given country. As with demand in general, trying to understand local demand only in terms of the perpetrators, without also examining the social, cultural and historical constructions and components that contribute to creating a 'market' for this crime, provides only a narrow understanding of the multiple forces driving this key factor in the commercial sexual exploitation of children.

Foreign demand is less extensive, but generally receives a higher profile, especially as the media gives much attention to cases of child sex tourism. Foreign demand also includes military personnel and aid workers who sexually exploit children in exchange for aid, security or money. More recently, organised sex tourism, especially in Asia and Central and South America, has increased the demand for sex with children. Foreign demand has also been spurred on by economic development policies that promote foreign investment, attracting expatriates and tourists.

In El Salvador, one-third of sexually exploited children between 14 and 17 years of age are boys. The median age for entering into prostitution among all children interviewed was 13 years.

Child pornography

The Optional Protocol defines child pornography as 'any representation, by whatever means, of a child engaged in real or simulated explicit sexual activities or any representation of the sexual parts of a child for sexual purposes'. Child pornography includes photographs, visual and audio representations and writing, and can be distributed through magazines, books, drawings, movies, video tapes, mobile phones and computer discs or files. Generally speaking, there are two categories of pornography: that which is not sexually explicit but involves naked and seductive images of children, and that which presents images of children engaged in sexual activity. The use of children in either way is sexual exploitation but existing international legal standards are limited to criminalising only the latter.

Child pornography exploits children in many different ways. Children may be tricked or coerced into engaging in sexual acts for the production of pornography, or images may be made in the process of sexually exploiting a child without the child's knowledge. These images are then distributed, sold or traded. Secondly, those who 'consume' and/or possess pornographic depictions of children are also exploiting the children, especially as the demand for such materials maintains the incentive to their production and consequently to the sexual abuse of the child. Thirdly, the makers of pornography commonly use their products to coerce, intimidate or blackmail the children used in the making of such material.

When investigators are able to identify children depicted in pornography, the abuser is commonly found to be a member or associate of the child's family or providing some care or guardianship. However, children who live or spend a lot of time on the streets, as well as children already forced into prostitution and children who are trafficked, are also at risk of being used in the production of child pornography.

ECPAT

The most obvious use of child pornography is sexual arousal and gratification. However, it is also used to validate certain beliefs and behaviour (e.g. the notion that it is 'OK' to have sex with children), establish trust among others interested in abusing children, gain entrance to private clubs, and to make a profit. At a societal level, child pornography, whether of real or simulated images of children, continues to cultivate a demand that involves sexual abuse and exploitation of children and is linked to the prostitution of children, child sex tourism, and the trafficking of children for sexual purposes.

New technologies and the growth of the Internet are creating more commercial opportunities for child exploiters and pornographers, as well as facilitating the development and extending the reach of distribution networks. Nowadays, child pornography is often produced and distributed using information and communication technologies (ICTs) and the Internet, as child pornographers use file sharing networks, news groups, peer-2-peer systems and other technologies to share and sell child pornography. These technologies facilitate organised sexual abuse and violence against children as perpetrated by networks of commercial buyers, sex tourists, paedophiles, traffickers, as well as more occasional forms of prostitution of children and young people such as *enjo kosai*, a Japanese term meaning 'compensated dating'. In addition, child sex exploiters use mobile phones and infiltrate chatrooms and other online social spaces to lure and groom children with the intent to abuse and exploit them, which poses many risks to children who use IT in their daily lives.

Through the use of digital graphics software, it is possible to combine two or more images into one, or distort pictures to create a completely new image, a process called morphing. Non-pornographic images of real children can be made to appear as pornography and pornographic images of 'virtual children' can be created. This raises new questions and issues, such as the age of a 'virtual child' and whether there can be a crime without a real victim. Child pornography is not just about images of naked children: the desire for sex with real children is maintained and promoted whether or not the image of the child is 'real', and there are clear links between child pornography and the sexual abuse of children. This is why materials such as cartoons and the Japanese comics 'manga', which depict children in sexual activities or in a highly sexualised manner, are also harmful.

The global distribution of child pornography over the Internet without uniform laws to protect children makes it difficult for national law enforcement authorities to prosecute offenders locally. As the Internet is not confined by national boundaries, harmonised legislation, international police cooperation and IT industry responsibility are required to tackle the problem.

In certain parts of the world, such as Eastern Europe and the CIS, there is a marked involvement of organised crime networks in the production and distribution of child pornography.

Several cases have highlighted how new technologies may be used to compound harm. In India, a teenage boy used his phone-camera to film sexual activity with his then girlfriend and sent the images to his friends via mobile phone. Eventually, the images were posted for sale online and videos were sold at local markets. In Canada, a teenage boy was charged with child pornography offences after posting naked images of his former girlfriend online after she broke up with him. The consequences for both girls were devastating and their humiliation is compounded by the awareness that the images had reached an extensive audience and will continue to do so long into the future.

Many countries still do not have effective legislation on child pornography. This legal vacuum creates a dangerous gap that exposes children to the risk of abuse, further increased by the impunity factor. Furthermore, each country has its own definition of what the age of consent to sexual activity is: in many cases, it is different from the age used in child pornography legislation, which can create problems in the application of child pornography laws.

Child sex tourism

Child sex tourism is the commercial sexual exploitation of children by people who travel from one location to another and there engage in sexual acts with minors. Often, they travel from a richer country to one that is less developed, but child sex tourists may also be travellers within their own countries or region. Sex tourism preys on sexual and economic inequality, and fosters other forms of commercial sexual exploitation of children such as child trafficking for sexual exploitation.

Child sex tourists come from all walks of life: they may be married or single, male or female, wealthy tourists or budget travellers. Some child sex tourists (preferential abusers and paedophiles) target children specifically; most, however, are situational abusers who do not usually have a sexual preference for children but take advantage of a situation in which a child is made available to them.

Anonymity, availability of children and being away from the moral and social constraints that normally govern behaviour can lead to abusive conduct in another country. Child sex exploiters may try to rationalise their actions by claiming that sex with a child is culturally acceptable in the place they are visiting, or that the money or goods exchanged benefit the child and community.

Destinations can change. When prevention and protection efforts are stepped up in one country, child sex tourists often shift to other destinations where it may be easier

ECPAT

or less risky to sexually exploit children. For instance, as Brazil and Thailand increase their vigilance, child sex tourism is rising in Ecuador, Cambodia, Vietnam and Indonesia. The opening up of transportation routes and markets, unregulated mass tourism development, and accentuated wealth discrepancies can also cause a shift in child sex tourism destinations, as in the case of North and South Eastern Europe, and Central America, which have experienced a growth in child sex tourism.

While tourism is not the cause of child sexual exploitation, child sex exploiters make use of the facilities offered by tour companies, hotels, resorts, restaurants, airlines and other transportation companies. Some businesses may be directly involved as well: for example, a hotel that turns a blind eye to sexual exploitation on its premises or travel agents that knowingly arrange sex tours abroad. The tourism industry is thus an important player and a valuable ally in the protection of children from sexual exploitation in tourism. Many travel and tourism organisations have recognised the key role they can play to better protect children, and are working together to combat child sex tourism.

Code of Conduct for the Protection of Children from Sexual Exploitation in Travel and Tourism

The Code of Conduct was initiated by ECPAT Sweden in 1998 in cooperation with Scandinavian tour operators and the United Nations World Tourism Organization (UNWTO). The Code encourages companies adopting it to commit themselves to:

1 Establish an ethical corporate policy against sexual exploitation of children;

2 Educate and train personnel in both the country of origin and travel destinations;

3 Introduce a clause in the contracts with suppliers, that makes a common repudiation of sexual exploitation of children;

4 Develop information and awareness-raising materials such as catalogues, brochures, posters, in-flight films, ticket slips, home pages etc;

5 Providing information to local 'key persons' at the destinations; and

6 Reporting annually on the implementation of these criteria.

Child marriage

Child marriage, or early marriage, involves the marriage of children and adolescents below the age of 18. It can be considered as a form of commercial sexual exploitation when a child is received and used for sexual purposes in exchange for goods or payment in cash or kind. Typically in such cases, parents or a family marry off a child in order to gain benefit or to support the family. While child marriages involve both boys and girls, it is more common for girls to be married to men who are significantly older than they are. In parts of West and East Africa and South Asia, marriages taking place before one or both individuals have reached puberty are not unusual, while marriage shortly after puberty is common among those living traditional lifestyles in the Middle East, North Africa and parts of Asia.

Early marriages threaten a child's human rights, including their right to education, good health and freedom of expression. In many cases, once married, an underage person can lose their status as a 'child' and whatever protection that affords nationally. Sometimes, the marriage is not intended to be a permanent union: in some countries, temporary marriages are possible via a short-term marriage contract, known as *siqueh* in the Middle East and North Africa. This, combined with a low legal age of marriage, means that it is possible to circumvent the illegal act of child prostitution.

There are a number of reasons why the tradition of child marriages continues. Fear of HIV infection has encouraged men in many countries to seek younger partners. Where poverty is acute, early marriage is seen as a strategy for economic survival. Early marriage may also be considered as a way to ensure that young girls are protected: families in rural Albania have encouraged their daughters to marry early to avoid the threat of kidnapping, while in northern Uganda and Somalia, families have married their daughters to militia members in exchange for protection for themselves and the girls.

Some children are forced into marriage by parents or families, which means that consent is made by somebody else on the child's behalf and the child does not have the opportunity to exercise the right to choose; other children are too young to make an informed decision. In these cases, early marriage is forced marriage. In its most extreme form, forced marriage is the result of abduction. In Uganda, young girls are abducted and forced to marry senior leaders in the guerilla movement known as the Lord's Resistance Army. These 'marriages' are used as rewards and incentives for male soldiers.

Many girls who are forced to marry early suffer from prolonged domestic violence. Furthermore, early marriage is often linked to wife abandonment, plunging young girls into extreme poverty and increasing the risk that they will be forced to enter the commercial sex trade in order to survive.

⇨ The above information is an extract from the ECPAT document *Questions & Answers about the Commercial Sexual Exploitation of Children* and is reprinted with permission. Visit www.ecpat.net for more information.

© ECPAT

ECPAT

Safeguarding children and young people from sexual exploitation

Information from the Department for Children, Schools and Families.

This article summarises what is known about the sexual exploitation of children and young people. It is important to recognise that the ways in which children and young people are exploited are constantly evolving. Practitioners should ensure that they have an up-to-date understanding of the pattern of sexual exploitation in their area.

Children's charities such as Barnardo's, the National Society for the Prevention of Cruelty to Children (NSPCC) and the Children's Society, law enforcement-led organisations such as the Child Exploitation and Online Protection Centre (CEOP) and the United Kingdom Human Trafficking Centre (UKHTC), Home Office pilot projects in Wolverhampton and Nottingham (1997) and the projects funded through the 'Tackling Prostitution – What Works?' initiative in Bristol and Sheffield, the work of the National Working Group for Sexually Exploited Children and Young People, as well as the Coalition for the Removal of Pimping (CROP) and the experiences of affected families and carers themselves, have all contributed to a greater understanding of how children and young people are sexually exploited, which should help LSCB partners identify those who are involved.

The nature of sexual exploitation

Any child or young person may be at risk of sexual exploitation, regardless of their family background or other circumstances. This includes boys and young men as well as girls and young women. However, some groups are particularly vulnerable. These include children and young people who have a history of running away or of going missing from home, those with special needs, those in and leaving residential and foster care, migrant children, unaccompanied asylum-seeking children, children who have disengaged from education and children who are abusing drugs and alcohol, and those involved in gangs.

Sexual exploitation can take many forms, from the seemingly 'consensual' relationship where sex is exchanged for attention, affection, accommodation or gifts, to serious organised crime and child trafficking. What marks out exploitation is an imbalance of power within the relationship. The perpetrator always holds some kind of power over the victim, increasing the dependence of the victim as the exploitative relationship develops. This article sets out some of the more common indicators found in cases of sexual exploitation.

Sexual exploitation involves varying degrees of coercion, intimidation or enticement, including unwanted pressure from their peers to have sex, sexual bullying (including cyber bullying), and grooming for sexual activity. Technology can also play a part in sexual abuse: for example, through its use to record abuse and share it with other like-minded individuals or as a medium to access children and young people in order to groom them. A common factor in all cases is the lack of free economic or moral choice.

> ## Barnardo's research in London from 2003-05 found 507 separate cases where child sexual exploitation was known or indicated

Many children and young people are groomed into sexually exploitative relationships but other forms of entry exist. Some young people are engaged in informal economies that incorporate the exchange of sex for rewards such as drugs, alcohol, money or gifts. Others exchange sex for accommodation or money as a result of homelessness and experiences of poverty.[1] Some young people have been bullied and threatened into sexual activities by peers or gangs which is then used against them as a form of extortion and to keep them compliant.[2]

Child sexual exploitation must be tackled effectively to prevent further problems in later life. Many adults involved in prostitution report difficult childhood histories that include domestic violence, familial child abuse, neglect, emotional abuse, time spent in care, disrupted schooling and low educational attainment. Many were also coerced into sexual exploitation as children or young teenagers.

Although the predominant evidence is of men sexually abusing children and young people, both men and women have been known to sexually exploit young men and young women. There is a presumption that children and young people are sexually exploited by people they do not know. However, evidence shows that they are often abused by 'boyfriends' or people with whom they feel they have a relationship. Professionals should also be alert to organised familial abuse or abuse within closed community groups, including sexual exploitation and the making and distribution of abusive images of children and trafficking of children into, within and out of the UK.

The perpetrators of sexual exploitation are often well organised and use sophisticated tactics. They are known to target areas where children and young people might gather without much adult supervision, such as shopping centres, cafes, takeaways, pubs, sports centres, cinemas, bus or train stations, local parks, playgrounds and taxi ranks, or sites on the Internet used by children and young people. The process of grooming may also be visible in adult venues such as pubs and clubs. In some cases perpetrators are known to use younger men, women, boys or girls to build initial relationships and introduce them to others in the perpetrator networks.

However, young people can also be sexually exploited by informal and unorganised groups of people. Children and young people, who are themselves the victims of exploitation, may introduce other young people to their abusers. This may not be a deliberate attempt to groom others into sexual exploitation, but rather a way of ensuring that their abuser's attention is deflected away from themselves. These children and young people are themselves victims and should not be prosecuted except as a last resort when other interventions have failed and there is an absolute need to protect others.

Similarly, children and young people may be groomed into 'party' lifestyles where they go to houses/flats with numerous men and other young women. These 'parties' often introduce children and young people to alcohol and drugs and offer a space to 'chill'. No single relationship is formed but a general network is created. Young men may be groomed through 'casual' social relationships formed at common meeting places with perpetrators introducing them to a 'macho' lifestyle of cafes/bars/arcades, etc. This may develop into socialising and making money from criminal activities such as shoplifting or car theft and be linked to other risky behaviours such as drinking and smoking. Many young men and boys who are being exploited will be secretive or ambiguous about their actual sexual orientation.

Other perpetrators will include friends, peers and friends of older siblings. In some cases, perpetrators may target young people through their parents or carers, by providing drugs, alcohol or money to the parents or carers. This can often mean that the parents or carers approve of the perpetrator as a potential boyfriend or girlfriend as they are trusted and needed by the family.

The majority of sexually exploited children and young people will be hidden from public view. They are unlikely to be loitering or soliciting on the streets of red light areas. Sexual exploitation is also more likely to take place in private premises than the more 'visible' saunas or massage parlours. Young people are groomed to be secretive about their meetings, which are usually arranged over mobile phones or the Internet, and the places and people they are meeting, so the activities are concealed from parents or carers. As sexual exploitation can be difficult to identify, and services working with children and young people may be unaware of the indicators of sexual exploitation, it is difficult to quantify the number of children and young people who are abused in this way.

Research and practice has, however, helped move the understanding of sexual exploitation by practitioners and policy makers away from a narrow view of seeing sexual exploitation as a young person standing on a street corner selling sex. As discussed, this is only a very small part of the picture. Policies and services therefore need to be broad enough to take into account a wide range of needs, local variations, different models of exploitation in different communities, and to identify children and young people at risk or who are victims of exploitation. This broad model also needs to be made clear in preventative education and in awareness-raising, early intervention through work in schools or targeted work with those missing school and their families. Similarly, early identification through health service provision for young people with sexual health or with behavioural difficulties and mental health problems is important.

Information on prevalence

Estimating the extent of child sexual exploitation nationally is difficult given the low awareness of the indicators of this abuse among service providers and the varying responses from local areas in terms of assessing their local situation. Research commissioned in 2002[3] following the publication of *Safeguarding Children Involved in Prostitution* reviewed local area take-up and found that children were known to suffer sexual exploitation in 111 (of the then 146) Area Child Protection Committee districts – with an average of 19 girls and three boys in each area.

Because of the grooming methods used by their abusers, it is very common for children and young people who are sexually exploited not to recognise that they are being abused

---

Smaller-scale studies since then suggest that this is a considerable under-estimate of the extent of the problem. Barnardo's research in London from 2003-05[4] found 507 separate cases where child sexual exploitation was known or indicated, with cases identified in every London borough. The total number of people estimated to be at risk across London was 1,002. CROP research, *Parents, Children and Pimps: Families speak out about sexual exploitation* (2005), considered 107 affected families between August 2002 and June 2005. A CEOP scoping study in 2007[5] found that 59 children of the 330 children profiled as potentially trafficked were identified or suspected as being sexually exploited. Of these, only one was a UK national and the rest were from Africa, Asia and Eastern Europe. In all situations, however, there are likely to be further numbers of children and young people, particularly boys and young men, who have not yet been identified.

Local Safeguarding Children Boards should put in place systems to monitor prevalence and responses to child sexual exploitation within their area. They should start from the basis that there is a problem to be addressed in their area – this would include gathering data from Board partners and other local stakeholders. Research undertaken by CEOP suggests that sexual exploitation does indeed take place in most areas across the country.[6]

It is also a crime that knows no borders and can be global in nature. It is important to respond with cross-border cooperation as it is possible that activity in one area may push perpetrators across a border, together with their young victims.

Sexual exploitation and wider harm to children and young people

Sexual exploitation is often linked to other issues in the life of a child or young person, or in the wider community context. It should not be regarded as an isolated issue. This is why a child who may be sexually exploited should be the subject of a holistic assessment of their needs, like any other child who may be in need, including those who may be suffering significant harm. Similarly, where a child has been identified as being at risk of significant harm and/or faces a complex range of difficulties, it is important that professionals consider whether they are also being sexually exploited.

Sexual exploitation has links to other types of crime. This includes:

➪ child trafficking (into, out of and within the UK).

➪ domestic violence.

➪ sexual violence in intimate relationships.

➪ grooming (both online and offline).

➪ abusive images of children and their distribution (organised abuse).

➪ organised sexual abuse of children.

➪ drugs-related offences (dealing, consuming and cultivating).

➪ gang-related activity.

➪ immigration-related offences.

➪ domestic servitude.

It also has links to other factors likely to affect the welfare of children and young people, including:

➪ running away from home and going missing.

➪ drug and alcohol misuse.

➪ sexual health.

➪ sexually risky behaviour.

➪ bullying.

➪ domestic servitude, neglect and violence.

➪ teenage pregnancy.

➪ long-term sexual, physical and psychological harm.

➪ forced marriage.

➪ self-harm and suicide.

And it can be related to other factors in the lives of children and young people:

➪ mental health issues.

➪ non-attendance at school and school phobia.

➪ learning disabilities.

⇨ being in residential and foster care.

⇨ forced isolation from community and family.

⇨ immigration status.

Attitudes of children and young people

Because of the grooming methods used by their abusers, it is very common for children and young people who are sexually exploited not to recognise that they are being abused. The needs of children and particularly of young people aged 16 and 17 years are likely to be overlooked for this reason. Although faced with limited choice, they may believe themselves to be acting voluntarily. It may take many weeks or months for practitioners who work with young people to build up their trust, help them to recognlse that they are being sexually exploited by challenging their perceptions with factual information, and overcome their resistance to interventions.

Impact of sexual exploitation on children and young people

Sexual exploitation can have a serious impact on the lives of children and young people. It can lead to difficulties in forming relationships with others, a lack of confidence or self-esteem and can affect their mental and physical health. Sexual exploitation can create feelings of worthlessness within children and young people, which can lead to acts of self-harm, including cutting themselves, overdosing and eating disorders. It can put the young person at increased risk of sexually transmitted infections including HIV, unwanted pregnancy and abortion, as well as long-term sexual and reproductive health problems. It can also ultimately impact on their parenting capacity in the future. Where children or young people manage to recover to some extent from sexual exploitation they will sometimes feel unable to stay in their local area because of the associations it holds for them (or because of very real threats from networks around their abusers), leading to family break-ups and isolation from family and friends.

Impact of child sexual exploitation on families

Sexual exploitation can have profound and damaging consequences for families, including parents and carers, siblings and extended members, and impact on their health, work life, family cohesion, economic stability and social life.[7] The use of technology can further complicate this, where abusive images have been posted on or shared through the Internet. Once these images have been distributed in this way there

is no control over who can access them, leading to the repeated victimisation of the child.

Targeting and grooming children and young people often has psychological implications for parents and other family members: life becomes difficult to manage and the stress of a situation which they do not understand can lead to despair, limiting their capacity to respond to the needs of their children and to deal with crises that occur as a result of the exploitation.

Parents and carers are often distraught, traumatised and under severe stress. They feel helpless and guilty for not being able to protect their children from sexual predators. They are likely to suffer verbal and physical aggression from the exploited child as well as violence or threats of violence from the perpetrators. Sexual exploitation of their children also places strain on family relationships. Sexual exploitation of one child in the family places other siblings at significant risk of being groomed and exploited. Siblings can be alienated and faced with bullying and their self-esteem and performance affected. Parents, carers and siblings can themselves suffer serious threats of abuse, intimidation and assault at the hands of perpetrators.

Notes

1 For a full description of different models of entry, and for local government and children's charities' interventions, and for specific work with young men and with black and ethnic minority communities, see Lowe K and Pearce JJ (2006) Special edition on 'Young People and Sexual Exploitation' *Child Abuse Review*, Vol 15. Further useful research is contained in: Pearce, JJ and Williams, M and Galvin, C (2002) *It's Someone Taking a Part of You: a study of young women and sexual exploitation*, London: The National Children's Bureau. ISBN 1-900990-83-0.

2 Sara Swann.

3 *Safeguarding Children involved in Prostitution, Guidance Review*, Sara Swann MBE and Valerie Balding (Department of Health, 2002).

4 *Meeting the needs of sexually exploited young people in London*, Zoe Harper and Sara Scott (Barnardo's, 2005).

5 *A Scoping Study into Child Trafficking in the UK* (CEOP, 2007).

6 Melrose, M with Barrett, D (2004) eds *Anchors in Floating Lives: Interventions with Young People Sexually Abused Through Prostitution* (Lyme Regis, Russell House Publishing).

7 *Parent Children and Pimps: Families speak out about sexual exploitation* (CROP, 2005).

⇨ The above information is an extract from the Department for Children, Schools and Families' report *Safeguarding Children and Young People from Sexual Exploitation: Supplementary guidance to Working Together to Safeguard Children*, and is reprinted with permission. Visit www.dcsf.gov.uk for more information on this and other related topics.

DEPARTMENT FOR CHILDREN, SCHOOLS AND FAMILIES

'They like us naïve': how teenage girls are groomed for a life of prostitution by UK gangs

13-year-old Emma was a happy child from a loving family when a gang of boys she met at a shopping centre introduced her to a charismatic older man. He plied her with gifts and drinks... then raped her and forced her into prostitution. Now aged 20 and in hiding from the gang, Emma talks candidly about how she was groomed – and how she is trying to help the growing number of others being picked out for a similar fate.

By Peter Stanford

Emma Jackson has a way of referring to her younger self that makes her teen years sound as though they were decades ago. 'My mum is my best friend,' she reflects at one point as we are talking. 'Now I'm older I'm really happy with that, but when I was 13, I saw things differently. I was much younger and I didn't want my mum at all. I just wanted my friends.'

The past sounds so far away that I have to keep reminding myself that Emma is still only 20. The transition from childhood to being an adult can be quick and is rarely smooth and painless, but Emma's exaggerated sense of the gap between 'before' and 'after' has been caused by something much more traumatic than regular teenage rebellion. For those friends she sought out so assiduously at 13 in the local shopping centre near her home in Yorkshire turned out not to be friends at all, but a well-organised gang of criminals, using teenage boys as bait to enable them to groom young, naïve girls like Emma for a life of prostitution.

From the distant vantage point of adulthood, she can now discern a disturbing pattern in how they treated her, but at the time it all felt spontaneous – and, at first, exciting. She was initially befriended by courteous, good-looking lads a few years' older than she was. Through them, she was introduced to their older friends, and finally, slowly and imperceptibly as she tells it, into the arms of what seemed a glamorous suitor called Tarik.

For a while Tarik was all rides in his smart car, gifts and drinks, cigarettes and drugs, which he encouraged her to try because, he reassured her, she was old enough, whatever her parents said. Then, overnight, he changed. Tarik was the gang's ringleader and one night dragged Emma into a seedy yard where he raped her. Once he had asserted his 'full control' over her by this violation, she was so confused by what had happened and terrified by his threats that she let him sell her on for sex with his middle-aged male clients.

'I never thought of myself as a prostitute,' she reflects, her down-to-earth voice strangely disengaged as she describes her own suffering, 'because, in my child's view of the world, prostitutes walked the streets, wore short skirts and high heels and I wasn't doing any of that. It is only now that I can see that, much as I wanted to believe Tarik had feelings for me, he didn't have any at all, except to make money out of me.'

Emma's case is not isolated – which is why she has agreed to relive the pain. There is an accumulation of evidence pointing to a growing problem with the sexual exploitation for criminal purposes of teenagers, both girls and boys. Barnardo's has recently produced a report, *Whose Child Now?*, which warns that children as young as ten are being 'brainwashed' and then sexually exploited by gangs in much the same fashion as Emma. It estimates, on the basis of work done by the charity in London, that 1,000 children in the capital alone are at risk of sexual exploitation in this way.

Hard figures for the UK as a whole are difficult to come by. One reason is that what happened to Emma is often conflated with the activities of gangs that traffic young sex workers into Britain for the sex industry, or with the use of the Internet by paedophiles for grooming gullible teenagers. Both these latter groups have been targeted by police and authorities in recent times, but the grooming of UK-born and based teenagers has received less attention.

Another complicating factor is that the assumption is made – including in the Barnardo's report – that the youngsters at risk from this criminal activity come from dysfunctional homes, or the estimated 80,000 under-16s who run away each year. Emma is anxious above all to dispel this impression. Her voice turns almost strident. 'Yes, there probably are a lot of girls who get involved because they come from broken homes, or are in care, but when you look at the whole situation, as I have, there are plenty who don't. The gangs know that if they take a girl from a nice family, she will probably be more naïve, not as streetwise as kids who have been in care. And because you are naïve, you are more trusting, easier to impress. They like that. It makes you easier to control. They'll have anybody – doctors' children, lawyers' children – anybody.'

Emma had, she says, a very happy childhood. 'I think of Dad as he was then, chunky, always dependable. If I was ever ill as a little kid, it was always Dad I wanted. Mum was always kind and loving, she protected us and encouraged us. The house was always comfortable, there was food on the table, we had nice clothes.'

By this stage of an interview, it would be usual to describe the person speaking and where we are talking, but Emma cannot be identified in this way. She is still in hiding from the gang that abused her. Her parents have given up their business – they used to run a local shop – and moved to a new area. Emma Jackson is a pseudonym.

Is she still frightened that the gang is looking for her? 'In a way, yes...' and then she pauses. 'And in a way, no,' she continues. 'It is children they scare, not grown women, and I am a grown woman now. So, yes, I could stand up to them if they turned up on my door, but that's not really what it is about. I don't want to be known for the rest of my life as the girl who was abused. It's not shame. I know now it wasn't my fault – though for a long time I thought it was. It is just that I don't want to be labelled a victim. I'm determined not to become a victim.'

It was soon after her 13th birthday that Emma went one Saturday with her school friend Joanne and some other classmates to a big shopping centre in the nearest town. 'None of us girls had what you'd call a boyfriend,' she explains, recapturing the innocence of the expedition, 'though there was lots of talk at school about who fancied who, all that sort of thing.'

Joanne, though, it seems, may have already been targeted by the gang and had been groomed to introduce Emma to Niv and Jay, two boys she'd already met there. 'I realised this was the first time I'd actually spoken directly to an Asian lad. What I was aware of, straight away, was how nice they looked. That made a real impact.'

A pattern developed. The girls would go into town by bus to meet Niv and Jay on Saturdays, then on some weekday evenings too. Emma's parents worked until late at their shop, and once her older brother had left to go to college, she had more freedom to stay out – as she had been unguardedly telling her new friends. 'Looking back,' she reflects, 'my family set-up was perfect to make me more vulnerable. Don't think for a minute I'm blaming Mum and Dad for working so hard. It is just that it was easy for me to tell lies, to pull the wool over their eyes. No wonder the bad guys wanted to know all about my family.'

Only at this stage, she didn't know they were bad. She thought they were genuinely interested in her. The fact that they told her so little about themselves in return rang no alarm bells, and so Niv and Jay started introducing her to older Asian friends of theirs. 'They're very clever. They get the younger ones to talk to you first. They know you've been taught if you come from a decent home not to talk to strangers, especially older men, but you will talk to boys just a bit older than yourself.'

And finally, along came Tarik. 'I liked his confidence – it was a quiet confidence, which is more impressive than shouting about it. And yes, I must say that seeing that other people admired him built him up in my eyes even more. There was a sort of power there.'

Others among Emma's friends felt that power, but were savvy enough to recognise it as malign. She didn't, and fell out with one who warned her off him. 'I suppose I felt different. Other girls in my class were hanging out with boys of 14, but I was getting to drive in smart cars with men. I felt my life was more exciting, better. That's how they got inside my mind.'

Tarik began reeling her in – asking her to run special errands for him, praising her in front of the group, even encouraging her to rebel against her parents' expectation that she would work occasionally in the evenings in their shop. 'They teach you to lie and deceive,' she recalls. 'It becomes normal.' And then, when he had driven a wedge between her and home, he suddenly turned on her.

Emma's account of the build-up to the rape is both heart-wrenching and convincing in every detail. She makes me understand, as she talks, how she was manipulated into that position. Where I struggle, though, as I tell her, is in understanding how, days after the rape, she went back to meet Tarik again. Surely, she should have learnt – in the most appalling way – that he was not a man she could trust. Perhaps she couldn't quite bring herself to tell her parents what had happened, but shouldn't some instinct have stopped her putting herself in danger again, or prompted her to seek help from other responsible

adults in her life, especially when Tarik began selling her to other men?

'They isolate you,' she explains, 'so I felt isolated from everyone around me. I believed that there was no one I could tell. They had convinced me that the gang were the only people I had. I remember at that time wanting someone to notice that I'd changed. My grades at school had gone from As to Ds and Es. I wanted someone to ask me what was happening, if there was a problem, and then I would have told them everything, but until someone asked me, I felt I couldn't say. That is how far they controlled me.'

And then there were the threats. 'They said that if I ever told anybody about what was happening they would firebomb my house, or rape my mother and make me watch. Tarik made me feel like a worm, or the s**t on his shoe. That's what I am, I thought, s**t on his shoe.'

So it went on for several months. 'I wanted it to stop, of course I did,' says Emma, 'but the way I look at it now is that it can take an adult who is in an abusive relationship several years to find the courage to escape, and I was only 13 and being mentally, physically and sexually abused. How was I going to have the courage to walk away?'

In the end, her mother found out. Neighbours began to report Asian men driving around the private housing development where she lived, looking menacing. Then one day Emma left her mobile phone on the kitchen table. It rang and her mother picked it up. The man's voice on the other end disturbed her, so she checked her daughter's messages. Knowing something was wrong – but not the full horror of it – her parents sat Emma down and asked what was going on, and out it all came. 'I'll never forget the look on my dad's face. It was like he'd been hit with a thunderbolt, his world crashing down. Then my big, burly dad was kneeling beside me, holding me, saying my name over and over, his voice breaking, choked with tears.'

The police were called, statements taken, medical investigations carried out – Emma counts herself fortunate not to have become pregnant or caught a sexually transmitted disease, since the men never used condoms. Tarik was arrested but denied everything. Emma was a teenage girl with a crush on him, making up tales to punish him for not being interested in her, he told police.

A prosecution was planned but then Joanne retracted the statement she had made supporting Emma. She had been there when her friend was first raped. There were plenty of threats being issued by the gang, so Emma simply accepts that Joanne was too scared. Which left it with her word against Tarik's. The case never made it to court.

'I don't regret that,' she says now. 'At the time I was in danger. I believe it was the right thing for me and my family. And I have found closure in other ways – by helping save other girls from being in that position.'

Emma's family relocated to Greece for a while, but found the strain of trying to build a new life there, after all that had happened, too much. Eventually they returned to another part of England. Her parents work, she says, but strictly nine to five and not in their own business. They want to be around for her, and, she admits, she continues to lean on them. 'They are very protective, but I like that. I like them sorting things out for me, even if I am being a bit childish. So they're the ones, for example, who have helped me do all the forms for going to college.'

Emma has resumed her education and is planning a career in the law. Forensics, in particular, interests her. Few of her fellow students will bring with them such a detailed knowledge of the workings – and shortcomings – of the law as she will. To which end, she also works with the Leeds-based campaigning group CROP – the Coalition for the Removal of Pimping – which was set up by the families of those affected by sexual exploitation of youngsters. Emma gives talks to parents facing the same horror that hers once did, and she is pushing for more police resources to be directed to tackling gangs like the one that groomed her.

In a pilot scheme in Blackburn in Lancashire, a joint venture by police and charities working in this field led, over a three-month period, to 60 charges of child abduction, rape and sexual activity with minors. It also produced a film to be shown to secondary-school children. 'I think there needs to be much more of that – warning them when they are 13 and so naïve and trusting about what can happen. And there needs to be more prosecutions. Tarik believed he was bigger than the law.'

While the gangs involved in grooming youngsters come from all sorts of backgrounds, Emma believes, on the basis of her own experience, that there was something in the culture of second- and third-generation men from the Indian sub-continent that drew them into such activities. 'White girls are classed as lower,' she says. 'These men class women as lower anyway, but white women are lower still. And in their tradition, girls become women at 12, so perhaps they didn't think they were doing wrong with me.'

As part of her campaigning, Emma is now publishing a memoir – *The End of My World*. It must have been painful to go back over everything that happened to her. 'Well, I've been doing that already, with counsellors and psychiatrists, and when I am speaking for CROP, but I wrote the book because I felt I was at the stage where I needed to move on, and it has helped me do that.'

And what of Tarik? She thinks for a long time before answering. 'I can't say I hate him. If anything I pity him. I feel like he'll never prosper in life. He'll always be an evil person.'

The End of My World, by Emma Jackson, is published on Thursday by Ebury Press, priced £6.99. For further information about CROP, visit cropuk.org.uk
31 January 2010

THE INDEPENDENT

Trafficked and exploited children

Information from the London Child Protection Committee.

Definitions of trafficking and exploitation

The two most common terms for the illegal movement of people – 'trafficking' and 'smuggling' – are very different. In human smuggling, immigrants and asylum seekers pay people to help them enter the country illegally; after which there is no longer a relationship. Trafficked victims are coerced or deceived by the person arranging their relocation. On arrival in the country of destination the trafficked child or person is denied their human rights and is forced into exploitation by the trafficker or person into whose control they are delivered.

The Palermo Protocol establishes children as a special case – any child transported for exploitative reasons is considered to be a trafficking victim – whether or not they have been deceived. This is partly because it is not considered possible for children to give informed consent.

Even when a child understands what has happened, they may still appear to submit willingly to what they believe to be the will of their parents.

How does trafficking happen?

Traffickers are known to recruit their victims using a variety of methods. Some children are subject to coercion, which could take the form of abduction or kidnapping. However, the majority of children are trapped in subversive ways:

⇨ Children are promised education or respectable work – in restaurants, as domestic servants etc.

⇨ Parents are persuaded that their children will have a better life elsewhere.

Many children travel on false documents and for those who do not, the traffickers usually throw away their identification papers.

Why do people traffick children?

Most children are trafficked and exploited for financial gain. This can take the form of payment from the child's parents, and in most cases the trafficker also receives payment from those wanting to exploit the child once in the UK. Some trafficking is by organised gangs, in other cases individual adults traffick children to the UK for their own personal gain. Exploitation includes children being used for:

⇨ sex work;

⇨ domestic servitude;

⇨ sweatshop and restaurant work, drug dealing and credit card fraud;

⇨ begging or pickpocketing;

⇨ benefit fraud;

⇨ drug mules or decoys for adult drug traffickers;

⇨ forced marriage (there were 240 reported cases in the UK in 2000-02, in 15% of cases the unwilling partner was male);

⇨ trade in human organs;

⇨ ritual killings.

Younger children are often trafficked to become beggars and thieves or for benefit fraud. Teenagers are often trafficked for domestic servitude, sexual exploitation and forced marriage.

Why is trafficking possible?

Factors in their own country which make children vulnerable to trafficking include:

⇨ Poverty: this is the root cause of vulnerability to exploitation in general. The recruiter's promise of work/income is seen by families as a possible escape route from impoverished circumstances; or at the very least one less mouth to feed.

Typical attitudes among children who have suffered commercial sexual exploitation

	GIRLS	BOYS
Fear	Pregnancy	Being/becoming gay
Feel	'Not themselves' Others see them as disgusting They are to blame They lack honour/dignity	That being with a paedophile is better than being with a homosexual Prostitution is acceptable if one is poor (wish to look after others more vulnerable)
Present	Consider prostitution as 'just a job' Need/want the money Like not being alone	Consider prostitution as 'just a job' Need/want the money Like not being alone Like/enjoy the work
Wish	Fantasise about 'real love' and lasting relationships (being 'rescued')	Want to get out / fantasise about 'caring' relationships

Source: Combating the trafficking in children for sexual purposes, ECPAT, 2006

LONDON CHILD PROTECTION COMMITTEE

- Lack of education: attendance at school has proven to be a key means of protecting children from all forms of exploitation, including trafficking. Traffickers promise education for children whose parents cannot afford to pay school fees or where schools are difficult to access or of poor quality.

- Discrimination: this can be based both on gender and ethnicity. In some cultures girls are expected to make sacrifices in terms of education and security for the benefit of the family; they represent less of an investment for the family because their contribution to the family will end when they leave to marry (and marriage itself may be too expensive for the family). Many trafficking victims are from minority communities who are socially discriminated against and disadvantaged in their own country.

- Cultural attitudes: traditional cultural attitudes can mean that some children are more vulnerable to trafficking than others: e.g. the caste system and a tradition of bonded labour in India puts tribal and low-caste children at risk.

- Dysfunctional families: children may choose to leave home as a result of domestic abuse and neglect.

- Political conflict and economic transition: conflict almost inevitably leads to large-scale people movements and the erosion of economic and social protection mechanisms, leaving children vulnerable.

- Inadequate local laws and regulations: trafficking involves many different events and processes and legislation has been slow to keep pace. Most countries have legislation against exploitative child labour, but not all have laws specifically against trafficking. Even where there is appropriate legislation, enforcement is often hampered by lack of prioritisation and ignorance of the law.

How are children brought to the UK?

Children enter the UK in two key ways: accompanied by adult/s or as unaccompanied minors.

Accompanied children

Very little is known about accompanied children, many of whom are brought in by adults either purporting to be their parents or stating that they have the parent's permission to bring the child. There are many legitimate reasons for children being brought to the UK, such as education, re-unification with family or fleeing a war-torn country.

Unaccompanied children

More is known about these children because they come to the notice of the authorities when they claim asylum. Although there appear to be some groups of children who do not seek help from the authorities, notably Chinese children who 'disappear' into the Chinese communities in the UK.

Many African children are referred to Children's Social Services after applying for asylum, and even register at school for up to a term, before disappearing again. It is thought that they are trafficked out of the UK to Europe. Children also come to London via Gatwick and Dover. However, recent experience is that as checks have improved at the larger ports of entry, traffickers are starting to use the smaller, less well-known ports of entry, such as Luton and Stansted airports.

Trafficking schemes

There are three phases in the trafficking process: the recruitment phase, the transit phase and the destination phase. The traffickers might be part of a well-organised criminal network, or they might be individuals helping out in only one of the various stages of the operation, such as the provision of false documentation, transport or a 'safe house'.

All children who have been exploited will suffer some form of physical or mental harm: usually, the longer the exploitation, the more health problems that will be experienced

---

The London 'ports' where children first present after entering the UK are the Waterloo Eurostar station, Heathrow airport and the Immigration and Nationality Directorate (IND) at Lunar House in Croydon.

What happens to children before they arrive in the UK?

Even before they travel, children can be subjected to various forms of abuse and exploitation to ensure that the trafficker's control over the child continues after the child is transferred to someone else's care.

- Voodoo is used to frighten children (usually girls) into thinking that if they tell anyone about the traffickers, they and their families will die.

- Confiscation of the child's identity documents.

- Threats of reporting the child to the authorities.

- Violence, or threats of violence towards the child.

- Threats of violence towards members of the young person's family.

⇨ Keeping the child socially isolated.

⇨ Keeping the young person locked up.

⇨ Some children are told that they owe large sums of money for their air fares, accommodation and food, and that they must work to pay this off – however they never earn enough to do this.

⇨ Depriving the child of money.

The impact of trafficking on children

Trafficked and exploited children are not only deprived of their rights to health and freedom from exploitation and abuse – they are usually also deprived of their right to an education and the life opportunities this brings.

Children in the sex industry are open to sexually transmitted infections, including HIV/AIDS; and for girls there is the risk of early pregnancy and possible damage to their reproductive health

---

Once children have been trafficked and exploited, they are vulnerable to:

Physical abuse and neglect

⇨ This can range from inappropriate chastisement to not receiving routine and emergency medical attention (partly through a lack of care about their welfare and partly because of the need for secrecy surrounding their circumstances).

⇨ Children in the sex industry are open to sexually transmitted infections, including HIV/AIDS; and for girls there is the risk of early pregnancy and possible damage to their reproductive health.*

⇨ Children frequently suffer physical beatings and rape.

⇨ Children also frequently suffer physical deprivations, including beatings, sensory deprivations and food deprivation.

⇨ Some trafficked children are subdued with drugs, which they then become dependent on. They are then effectively trapped within the cycle of exploitation, continuing to work in return for a supply of drugs.

⇨ Children often develop alcohol addictions.

⇨ Victims can suffer physical disorders such as skin diseases, migraine, backache etc.

* See also the London procedure *Safeguarding Children Abused through Sexual Exploitation*, LCPC, 2006.

Psychological harm

⇨ Children become disorientated after leaving their family environment, however impoverished and difficult, and arriving in the western world. This disorientation can be compounded for some children who have to assume a new identity or have no identity at all.

⇨ Children can be isolated from the local community in the UK by being kept away from school and because they cannot speak English.

⇨ Trafficked and exploited children are living in fear both of the adults who have control of them and of the discovery of their illegal immigration status.

⇨ Victims lose their trust in all adults.

⇨ Trafficked and exploited children will all suffer from a form of post-traumatic stress relating to their sense of powerlessness and the degree of violence they experienced at the hands of their traffickers, which can be extreme.

⇨ Many trafficked and exploited children develop dependant relationships with their abusers.

⇨ They suffer flashbacks, nightmares, anxiety attacks, irritability and other symptoms of stress, such as nervous breakdowns.

⇨ Trafficked and exploited children experience a loss of ability to concentrate.

⇨ They can become anti-social, aggressive and angry, and/or fearful and nervous – finding it difficult to relate to others, including in the family and at work.

⇨ Victims have very low self-esteem and believe that the experience has 'ruined' them for life, psychologically and socially. They become depressed, and often suicidal.

⇨ The children worry about people in their families and communities knowing what has happened to them, and become afraid to go home.

All children who have been exploited will suffer some form of physical or mental harm: usually the longer the exploitation, the more health problems that will be experienced. Although in some cases, such as contracting AIDS or the extreme abuse suffered by Victoria Climbié, fatal damage happens very quickly.

⇨ The above information is an extract from the London Child Protection Committee's document *London Procedure for Safeguarding Trafficked and Exploited Children*, and is reprinted with permission. Visit www. londoncpc.gov.uk for more information om this and other related topics.

© London Child Protection Committee

LONDON CHILD PROTECTION COMMITTEE

Fifth of Britons unknowingly aid child trafficking, according to survey

⇨ **Buying pirate DVDs can benefit 'slave trade'.**

⇨ **Third of adults not aware of extent of the problem.**

By Robert Booth

More than a fifth of Britons may be unknowingly contributing to child trafficking, a survey published today reveals.

People who buy pirate DVDs and roses from street vendors, smoke home-grown cannabis, give money to child beggars and use prostitutes may be supporting what the United Nations has described as 'a modern day slave trade', says research published by ECPAT, the international campaign against the sexual exploitation of children.

According to the survey, published at the launch of a nationwide campaign to raise awareness, 89% of those questioned were not aware that their activities may be contributing to illegal businesses run by networks who smuggle children from China, Africa and Afghanistan.

'If you engage in these activities then you are supporting the illegal economy and that includes trafficking,' said Chris Beddoe, chief executive of ECPAT UK. 'Children are trafficked into the UK every day, across big cities and small towns. They have their identities removed, they are raped, beaten and forced to work in deplorable conditions.'

The Home Office's UK Human Trafficking Centre received three reports a week about children smuggled into the UK between April and June, the first three months of operation of a national referral mechanism, and this is thought to represent just a fraction of the cases.

Detective Inspector Gordon Valentine, who heads Operation Palladin, the Metropolitan Police's specialist anti-child trafficking team, said they have worked on cases where DVD-selling rings were linked to child traffickers. Afghan children are often used to work in illegal indoor cannabis farms and girls from Africa, China and Eastern Europe are known to have been trafficked into prostitution.

According to the survey conducted across 17 UK cities, a third of adults were not aware of the extent of child trafficking in the UK and a third believe trafficked children only end up in foreign countries.

'There has been a culture of disbelief,' said Jan Buckingham, values director at the Body Shop which is helping to fund ECPAT UK as part of the campaign. 'People don't see that children are being trafficked into the UK. They turn a blind eye.'

The campaign will be backed by posters in 300 Body Shop windows across the UK. The UK appears to be a hub for an international trade, with children from 52 nations trafficked in a single year, but calls for better care for victims have been resisted by the Government, according to ECPAT UK.

The report came amid warnings that the global economic crisis is set to increase the international trade. A parallel report by ECPAT, which works in 75 countries, predicted that with a further 65 million people falling below the poverty line, more families will be tempted to place their children in exploitative situations.

It said budgets for education of girls may be the first to be cut in the downturn by some governments, leaving them vulnerable to traffickers. The report's authors also anticipate that brothel customers will move downmarket to save money, which may put more trafficked children at risk.

⇨ This article was amended on Friday 14 August 2009. We inadvertently included Africa in a list of countries. This has been corrected.

14 August 2009

THE GUARDIAN

Concerns raised over low number of convictions for child trafficking

Information from Children & Young People Now.

By Neil Puffett

Less than half of prosecutions for human trafficking offences, including the exploitation of children for sex or crime, result in a conviction, CYP Now has learned.

From April 2007 to March 2009, there was a total of 201 prosecutions, while between January 2007 and December 2009 there were 73 convictions for human trafficking in the UK, making the conviction rate for cases prosecuted 45 per cent at best.

This is significantly lower than conviction rates for rape, traditionally seen as a low mark, which in 2008 stood at 58 per cent.

The statistics are set out in a letter seen by CYP Now from Security Minister Baroness Neville-Jones to crossbench peer Lord Elystan Morgan.

Less than half of prosecutions for human trafficking offences, including the exploitation of children for sex or crime, result in a conviction, CYP Now has learned

Christine Beddoe, director of End Child Prostitution, Child Pornography and the Trafficking of Children for Sexual Purposes (ECPAT UK), said the conviction rate for child trafficking is a profound problem. She cited current legislation as an issue, as prosecutors have to prove double intent: by the offender to move a person across a national border, as well as intent to exploit them.

'Children's cases are not being pursued and we are concerned about that,' she said. 'It is not simply about police action, it is about what the Crown Prosecution Service is doing once they have evidence. They are going for lesser offences and not prosecuting more difficult trafficking charges.'

CYP Now reported concerns last week that vulnerable children who have been trafficked are receiving substandard care because of a lack of leadership at central government level.

Beddoe said levels of care can also suffer as a result of prosecutors opting to pursue lesser charges.

'If a child trafficker is prosecuted for a lesser offence, the child is not afforded the same level of support and witness protection, which can mean a higher risk of the child being re-trafficked,' she said.

A Home Office spokesperson said: 'Combating human trafficking is a key priority for the Government, which is committed to tackling organised crime groups that profit from this human misery.

'The proposed National Crime Agency will help combat organised crime, including trafficking, more effectively.'

7 September 2010

⇨ The above information is reprinted with kind permission from Children & Young People Now. Visit www.cypnow.co.uk for more information.

© *Children & Young People Now*

Questions and answers about child soldiers

Who are child soldiers?

The Coalition to Stop the Use of Child Soldiers considers the term 'child soldier' to be equivalent to the following description of children associated with armed forces or groups:

> A child associated with an armed force or armed group refers to any person below 18 years of age who is, or who has been, recruited or used by an armed force or armed group in any capacity, including but not limited to children, boys and girls, used as fighters, cooks, porters, spies or for sexual purposes. It does not only refer to a child who is taking, or has taken, a direct part in hostilities.
>
> (Source: Paris: *Principles and guidelines on children associated with armed forces or armed groups*, UNICEF, February 2007)

Child soldiers perform a range of tasks including participation in combat, laying mines and explosives; scouting, spying, acting as decoys, couriers or guards; training, drill or other preparations; logistics and support functions, portering, cooking and domestic labour; and sexual slavery or other recruitment for sexual purposes.

Why are girls considered child soldiers? Don't they just accompany the men and boys who do the fighting?

Girls usually fulfil multiple roles. While they are frequently recruited and used for sexual purposes, they are virtually always also involved in other military tasks, including combat, laying explosives, portering and performing domestic tasks.

How many child soldiers are there?

It is not possible to give a global figure for the number of child soldiers at any one time.

The reason that exact figures cannot be calculated are various. For example, military commanders frequently conceal children or deny access to observers. Armed groups frequently operate in dangerous, inaccessible zones to which observers do not have access and

many children perform support roles and are therefore not visible in military operations.

The way in which children are recruited also prevents accurate documentation. Children are recruited both formally and informally. In some situations they stay in their communities and report only when required and often for short periods of time, for example when fighting escalates or to build strength while negotiating a demobilisation package. Child soldiers also shift between groups or are released and then recruited by a different group. Many children are killed or die of injuries sustained or illnesses caused by the hardships of military life. Child soldiers often reach the age of 18 while in the ranks and are no longer considered children. The years spent as a child soldier then become invisible.

While thousands of children have come out of fighting forces in the last five years as wars ended in countries such as Angola, Liberia, Sierra Leone and Sri Lanka, thousands more have been drawn into new conflicts, for example in Chad, Cote d'Ivoire and Sudan.

In countries such as Colombia, the Democratic Republic of Congo and Myanmar (Burma), there has been little change and thousands of children continue to be used as soldiers.

Africa has the largest number of child soldiers. Child soldiers are being used in armed conflict in Central African Republic, Chad, Democratic Republic of Congo, Somalia and Sudan

Which country or region has the worst record for using child soldiers?

Unfortunately child soldiers exist in all regions of the world and in almost every country where there is armed conflict.

Africa has the largest number of child soldiers. Child soldiers are being used in armed conflict in Central African Republic, Chad, Democratic Republic of Congo, Somalia and Sudan.

In Asia, thousands of children are involved in fighting forces in active conflict and ceasefire situations, although government refusal of access to conflict zones has made it impossible to document the numbers involved. Myanmar is unique in the region, as the only country where government armed forces forcibly recruit and use children between the ages of 12 and 18. Child soldiers also exist in Afghanistan, Bangladesh, India, Indonesia, Nepal, the Philippines and Thailand, where they are mainly associated with armed opposition groups, factional or clan-based groups or groups composed of ethnic or religious minorities.

In the Middle East, child soldiers are reportedly used in Iran, Iraq and Israel, and the Occupied Palestinian Territories and in tribal groups in Yemen.

In Latin America, up to 14,000 children are estimated to be involved with armed political groups and army-backed paramilitaries in Colombia.

In Europe, under-18s are believed to be involved in Turkey and a range of armed groups in the Chechen Republic of the Russian Federation, although the numbers are impossible to establish given the lack of information available.

Why is the minimum recruitment age for child soldiers set at 18? Surely in many 'non-western' societies children assume 'adult' responsibilities far below this age?

The Coalition to Stop the Use of Child Soldiers bases its work on international legal standards for child protection. The Convention on the Rights of the Child sets the age of majority at 18 years. It states that children and youth below 18 require special protection because of their physical and mental immaturity. Virtually all nation states have pledged to implement the provisions of the Convention.

The Optional Protocol to the Convention on the Rights of the Child on the involvement of children in armed conflict came into force in February 2002. It deals specifically with the use of child soldiers. It bans the direct use of all children under the age of 18 in hostilities and prohibits all military use of under-18s by non-governmental armed groups. While government armed forces are permitted to recruit volunteers from the age of 16, they must take steps to ensure that the recruitment is genuinely voluntary. Many 'non-western' states were involved in drafting and negotiating the Optional Protocol and many have pledged to abide by its terms and to end the use of child soldiers.

The governments of Canada, France, Germany, the UK and the USA continue to recruit under-18-year-olds into their armed forces

There is continuing debate about the age of adulthood in 'western' and non-western' countries. For example, the governments of Canada, France, Germany, the UK and the USA continue to recruit under-18-year-olds into their armed forces, although they are not allowed to vote. In some Middle Eastern countries on the other hand, the age of majority is higher than 18 years. In many countries where children are recruited – either legally or illegally – families, communities, activists, academics, doctors, lawyers and former child soldiers themselves have spoken out against the practice. They have argued for laws and other measures to protect children from the dangers and trauma of involvement in hostilities or other military activity.

Does the Coalition to Stop the Use of Child Soldiers support the recruitment of under-18-year-olds into government armed forces?

No. The Coalition to Stop the Use of Child Soldiers

campaigns for a complete prohibition of all recruitment and use of under-18s for military purposes by any armed force. Even if they are not sent to fight, young recruits in government armed forces are frequently exposed to bullying and other forms of physical or sexual abuse, hazardous training activities, and to harsh discipline and difficult living conditions.

Some child soldiers are known to have committed human rights atrocities. Shouldn't they be punished for such crimes?

Child soldiers, even those who have committed human rights abuses, should be treated first and foremost as victims of adult crimes – the prosecution of those who unlawfully recruited and used them should be prioritised.

However, there will be cases where a child soldier was clearly in control of his or her actions, was not coerced, drugged or forced into committing atrocities. In such cases, not holding children accountable may deny justice to the victims. Acknowledgement or atonement, including in some instances prosecution, may be an important part of personal recovery and may contribute to successful reintegration of former child soldiers into their families, communities and society at large. However, in any criminal justice process involving a former child soldier, international standards on juvenile justice must be adhered to.

Most child soldiers are used by non-governmental armed political groups. How can they be stopped from using child soldiers?

Non-governmental armed groups are not bound by international law in the same way as governments. However, child soldier recruiters may face prosecution by the International Criminal Court, established in 1998. The statute of the court defines the use of children under 15 in hostilities as a war crime. The court announced its first investigations in 2003, in the Democratic Republic of Congo and Uganda, where child soldiers have been extensively used by armed groups. In 2006 it prosecuted a Congolese warlord for recruitment of child soldiers.

The Special Court for Sierra Leone issued its first indictments in 2003, including against former Liberian president Charles Taylor. The indictments included charges of recruiting or using children under the age of 15 in hostilities. The court was established in 2002 to prosecute those suspected of responsibility for war crimes and crimes against humanity during the 1991-2002 war.

Prosecutions of child recruiters may serve as a deterrent to armed groups in future. Some armed groups are seeking international legitimacy and support for their political objectives. Negative publicity arising from child soldier use might undermine such support and lead to pledges and action to stop the practice. Armed groups may also respond to pressure from governments tacitly supporting their activities or providing military or other assistance. In some cases armed groups may be open to negotiations with governments or the UN aimed at demobilising child soldiers. If children continue to be used, the Coalition to Stop the Use of Child Soldiers considers that the international community should act decisively with targeted sanctions and prosecutions to stop the operations of such groups.

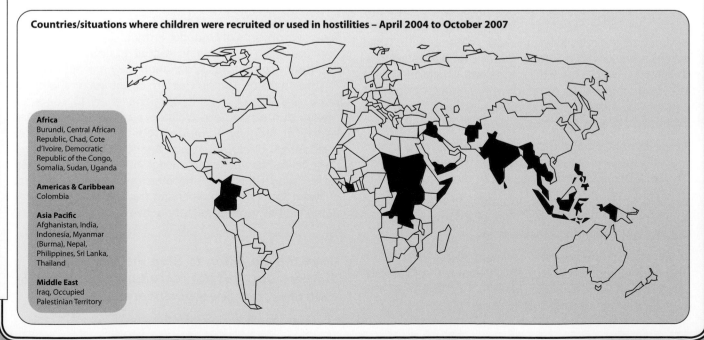

Countries/situations where children were recruited or used in hostilities – April 2004 to October 2007

Africa
Burundi, Central African Republic, Chad, Cote d'Ivoire, Democratic Republic of the Congo, Somalia, Sudan, Uganda

Americas & Caribbean
Colombia

Asia Pacific
Afghanistan, India, Indonesia, Myanmar (Burma), Nepal, Philippines, Sri Lanka, Thailand

Middle East
Iraq, Occupied Palestinian Territory

Fighting isn't just for boys: girls go to war

An extract from the Women's Refugee Commission's report Refugee Girls: The Invisibles Faces of War.

> 'I'm a 14-year-old girl fighting with rebel troops in Sri Lanka, who kidnapped me when I was only eight. I didn't know why I had to fight government soldiers. A rebel leader told me that I had to kill as many soldiers as possible for independence. I just want to be a good girl and have a normal life.'
>
> *14-year-old girl, Sri Lanka*
>
> 'I was captured in Lofa County by government forces. The forces beat me, they held me and kept me in the bush. I was tied with my arms kept still and was raped there. I was 14 years old... After the rape I was used in the fighting to carry medicine.'
>
> *Evelyn, recruited in Liberia by government forces at age 14*

There are at least 300,000 child soldiers in the world today. One in three is a girl.

In Liberia, children as young as seven have been found in combat, while in Cambodia, a survey of wounded soldiers found that 20 per cent of them were between the ages of ten and 14 when recruited. Since 2002, the Lord's Resistance Army, a rebel group in northern Uganda, has abducted more than 8,400 children, many of whom have been forced to attack their own families, neighbours and villages.

Human Rights Watch has estimated that in Colombia, up to 20 per cent of paramilitary forces are child soldiers – roughly 11,000 to 14,000 children – and anywhere from one-quarter to one-half of them are 'recruited' girls, some as young as eight years old

One major study estimated that between 1990 and 2003, girls were part of fighting forces in 55 countries. Human Rights Watch has estimated that in Colombia, up to 20 per cent of paramilitary forces are child soldiers – roughly 11,000 to 14,000 children – and anywhere from one-quarter to one-half of them are 'recruited' girls, some as young as eight years old.

Sometimes girls caught in war-torn regions choose to enlist for protection in response to threats of violence. Among Liberian girl ex-combatants, the number one reason given for joining a fighting force was for protection from sexual violence. A number of Liberian girls reported joining fighting forces after government forces had killed their parents and raped the girls in their families.

Girls sometimes join the fighting forces because they passionately believe in the cause they are fighting for. Voluntary enlistment by children is hardly the norm, however. Most girls who end up as members of armed groups are either abducted or physically coerced. Many are raped and sexually assaulted at the time of their abduction. Although their abductors are more likely to be rebel forces, thousands of girl soldiers are also recruited into service by government troops.

Boys and girls may both receive weapons and military training and engage in front-line combat, and both are often sent ahead to de-mine contaminated areas. They

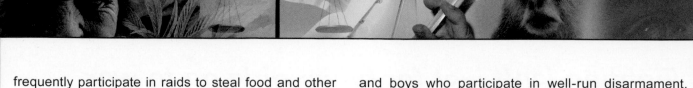

frequently participate in raids to steal food and other supplies, and to abduct other children. Both may work as porters, helping to carry food, weapons and loot, as their armed groups tend to be constantly on the move. And both are often put to work in illicit commercial operations, such as mineral mines, rubber plantations and logging operations, as well as forced to act as human 'mules', carrying weapons, gems, drugs and other illicit goods.

But because of their gender, girls are frequently expected to provide an additional service to armed groups. They serve as sex slaves, their young bodies offered up as inexpensive rewards. In conflict regions throughout the world, girl soldiers are commonly divided up and allocated to soldiers and rebels to serve as their 'wives'.

Large numbers of girl soldiers become girl mothers. They are forced to fight with infants on their backs, their babies heavily drugged to ensure that they remain quiet

Child combatants – boys and girls alike – suffer chronic and severe physical and mental health problems and injuries. Many child combatants are regularly supplied with opiates, marijuana, cocaine and other drugs to make them more malleable and fearless.

Girl combatants face unique health issues because of the sexual violence they experience. Health complications arising from pregnancy, delivery, abortion or miscarriage, often aggravated by the absence of any healthcare as well as an acute lack of knowledge about reproductive health on the part of young girl soldiers, are common. Girls are also susceptible to contracting HIV and other sexually transmitted infections.

Large numbers of girl soldiers become girl mothers. They are forced to fight with infants on their backs, their babies heavily drugged to ensure that they remain quiet. Girl soldier mothers who return from military captivity face rejection and stigmatisation by their families and communities, and threats and abuses against them and their children. They are less likely to return to school and have their children attend school. Their prospects for marriage are reduced. In addition, they are often excluded from rehabilitation and reintegration programmes, which help children adjust to civilian life and help ensure they are accepted by their families and communities.

Former girl soldiers, especially those who bear children, are among the most invisible of girls.

Yet, with the right help, former child soldiers, girls and boys who participate in well-run disarmament, demobilisation and reintegration (DDR) programmes and have access to education or skills training can rejoin their families and become valuable members of their communities. Some success has been reported when non-governmental organisations work closely with community leaders, stressing forgiveness for, and acceptance of, children who had been forced into their roles as soldiers. Traditional cleansing and healing ceremonies also appear to increase community acceptance of, and trust in, the children.

⇨ The above information is an extract from the Women's Refugee Commission's report *Refugee Girls: The Invisible Faces of War*, and is reprinted with permission. Visit http://womensrefugeecommission.org for more.

WOMEN'S REFUGEE COMMISSION

Rebuilding the lives of Congo's child soldiers

For Congo's child soldiers, brutalised and forced to kill, rehabilitation is a long journey. Yet in war-ravaged eastern Congo one transitional centre is slowly helping them rebuild their lives. Mary Riddell sees it at work, and talks to Congo's president, Joseph Kabila.

Gilbert did not mean to kill anyone. He did not even intend to go to war. He was ten when a relative enlisted him in a rebel army in eastern Congo and 12 when he led a raid in which his cousin died. 'I was ordered to kill the son of the leader in my village. I was put in charge of the group, and ordered to fire as people fled. The leader was my uncle; his boy was six years old.'

If Gilbert wished, he could make excuses for what he did. He could say, truthfully, that he would have been executed if he had failed to obey orders. In the frenzy of battle, he cannot even be sure whose bullet dealt the mortal wound. But, as the appointed leader, he shoulders all blame for an atrocity whose legacy he will never escape.

> **About 5.4 million people have died in the war that has ravaged Congo for the majority of Gilbert's lifetime. About 54 per cent of children here live in poverty; one-third will not finish primary school**

Gilbert is 16 now, and we meet in the transitional centre for former child soldiers where he has lived since UN peacekeepers rescued him two years ago. He is a solemn boy with a laddered yellow T-shirt and a face turned old by sorrow.

He has not told his story before, and he volunteers the information slowly. At first, he was enrolled by his relative in the CNDP (National Congress of the Defence of the People), the militia headed by Laurent Nkunda, now being held in a Rwandan jail. Gilbert was tortured before fleeing into the arms of Pareco, a rival rebel group and another finishing school for juvenile killers.

By some fluke, Gilbert did not die in the crossfire between the two militias. One bullet hole is gouged in his neck close to the carotid artery; a second shot hit his groin. 'I was near a hospital, and a doctor bound up the wounds. But I wasn't allowed to stay. After a few hours I was back in the forest. There were constant battles and, by the end, I was fighting every day. Then someone brought me here.'

'I cannot go back to school. I have already reached adult age. I would love to see my family but I cannot go home to my village because of what I have done. My brother came to see me once, and I asked if I could return. He said that if I did, my old friends would kill me.' I ask if he misses anything about being a soldier, and he says, 'I hate violence. But I think sometimes of my *mitraillette* [sub-machine gun]. I took it everywhere with me.'

Far from being the boast of a juvenile Rambo, this seems more like the nostalgia a normal adolescent might feel for an old toy. Gilbert has no other relics of childhood to cling to and no good future to embrace. He is a child of modern Congo: his story typical of a thousand others.

Congo should be a country of plenty. It possesses vast mineral wealth and its fertile land could feed the whole of Africa, but conflict and recession have left a nation the size of western Europe close to bankruptcy. About 5.4 million people have died in the war that has ravaged Congo for the majority of Gilbert's lifetime. About 54 per cent of children here live in poverty; one-third will not finish primary school.

These are the lucky ones. More than a fifth of children die in infancy, and 45,000 under-fives perish each year from avoidable causes. At the root of disease and exploitation is the internecine conflict whose fighters – easy to snatch and simple to train – are often under ten years old. About 31,000 children have been demobilised from Congo's battlefields since 1999, but at least 8,000 are still being used as combatants, porters and sex slaves.

The transitional centre where Gilbert lives stands in Goma, the major town of the eastern Kivu provinces. A row of shabby single-storey buildings is divided into classrooms and dormitories, where the 311 boys sleep, six to a room, in wooden bunk beds. The five girls who stay here have a room annexed to the director's office to give them some vestige of privacy and extra protection.

A large playground running the length of the compound is bounded by high walls and security gates designed to keep intruders out. Although the layout suggests a halfway house between a boarding school and a young offender institution, the noise of boys at play reflects the joy of freedom.

This centre, set up in 2005 by a Congolese NGO called Cajed (Concert d'Actions pour Jeunes et Enfants Défavorisés) and financially backed by UNICEF, is one of several similar institutions scattered across the country. UNICEF helped reintegrate 4,657 child soldiers into their communities last year at a cost of $700 per

THE TELEGRAPH

child, but lack of funding means that a backlog of 3,000 youngsters are denied the specialist help on offer here.

UNICEF's regional head, Julien Harneis, urges all armed groups to give up their child soldiers. 'The conflict is causing untold humanitarian suffering and gross violations of children's rights,' he says.

Few understand such attrition better than Fidele Rutabagisha, the director of the Goma centre. He and his 17 staff are used to dealing with adolescents whose bitter experiences mean that their moods seesaw between glee and anger. From the moment they are referred to his care, Rutabagisha embarks on a regime of 'peaceful rehabilitation'.

'These children are used to the field of battle,' he says. 'They have to live together in peace. First we give them clothes, blankets and sabots [plastic clogs]. Then we divide them into "family" units. They eat together and take care of their surroundings. They learn self-respect and *la vie morale*.'

Discipline is key to the curriculum. The children are woken at 6am and given an hour in which to wash, tidy their rooms and speak to their 'families'. Breakfast, which they prepare themselves, is from 7am to 8am. The rest of the day is divided into hour-long slots devoted to science, maths, music, sport and languages. 'Morality' lessons focus on community life, courtesy and self-respect.

Outside counsellors are brought in to treat children with emotional and mental health problems, and pupils are gradually allowed out to mingle with townspeople. Some transfer to a halfway house to be taught alongside 'normal' children: Oxfam, in conjunction with Cajed, offers counselling and training in carpentry, electronics, cooking and sewing to help teenagers back into the community.

Last year the joint programme arranged 558 homecomings. For the less fortunate, the only prospect is life with a host family, or a lone existence for those nearing adulthood. For the third of children who will never go home, the joy of others is sometimes hard to bear. Rutabagisha shows me a room damaged in a recent fracas. 'Some of the boys broke windows and smashed the roof. They were angry that no families could be found for them.'

Rutabagisha's pupils, who range from eight to 16, have experiences to chill an adult soul. Some were abducted from loving families. Others were persuaded by influential adults that life as a soldier would be well-paid and easy. Guelord, 15, was invited to a relative's home to meet his older cousin's new bride. 'But there was no wife. My cousin said, "Get into this uniform. Here's a gun." I was trapped. I thought I could stay for a few days and then escape, but they paraded me as a soldier, and I could not go back after that. I did three years.

'The children serving with Pareco were on guard all night; many were assassinated by the CNDP, our enemy. If you made one mistake, you would be killed by your superiors. I did not kill anyone, but I wounded an older boy in an attack on the CNDP. I watched my bullet go into his leg, and I was frightened I would die, like many of my friends.'

Like many of the children here, Guelord was rescued by the UN. As yet no family has been found for him, but he hopes he will one day become a street trader or, if he is lucky, a shopkeeper.

Unlike the boys in the centre, Niclette never wanted to be here. She is 17, and five months pregnant. She went to war with her husband, who is in his thirties; not to fight, but because he told her they should be together. When a child protection team brought her here, she was distraught.

'No one bothered me when I was in the army. I was by my husband's side, and I was not prepared for this. I didn't know we would have to separate. I want and hope to see my husband again.'

Niclette cannot go home to her parents in Masisi, 30 miles away, because she is now the property of her husband. 'He gave my father and mother three goats as a dowry when we married, which means they cannot take me back.' So she waits here, unsure what will happen to her or her child. 'I hope my baby will have the life of my parents, who grow beans and manioc,' she says.

The civil war that defines modern Congo traces back to the country's independence in 1960. A military coup by Joseph Mobutu in 1965 ushered in an age of corruption fuelled by the country's mineral wealth. In 1997 neighbouring Rwanda invaded to flush out Hutu rebels, allowing anti-Mobutu insurgents to oust the president and install Laurent Kabila in his place. In the ensuing fracas, Rwanda and Uganda tried to unseat Kabila, who was shot dead by one of his bodyguards in 2001, leaving his son to assume the presidency. A close-run election in 2006 established Joseph Kabila as Congo's first democratically-appointed leader.

Now, he tells me in a rare interview, his country is moving away from war. But the calm he proclaims is highly provisional. Earlier this year Kabila joined forces with his enemy, the Rwandan president Paul Kagame, to attack the rebel FDLR, made up of Hutu extremists who fled to Congo after orchestrating the Rwandan genocide in 1994.

In return, Laurent Nkunda – the CNDP leader who plotted to overthrow Kabila – was arrested and placed in custody by Rwanda, which had regarded him as an ally until international backers threatened to withdraw aid as a protest against the regime's perceived approval of Nkunda's killing sprees. This win-win deal, heralded as a great move towards peace by both leaders, has

THE TELEGRAPH

not so far benefited Congo's beleaguered children. A few weeks after the end of hostilities, Oxfam reported that the FDLR were regrouping and that 250,000 more people had been displaced. As violence flared again, the charity repeated the call for the world to act and, in particular, to muster the long-promised 3,000 extra troops to boost MONUC, the UN's biggest but enfeebled peacekeeping force.

About 31,000 children have been demobilised from Congo's battlefields since 1999, but at least 8,000 are still being used as combatants, porters and sex slaves

---

Kabila refuses to acknowledge the frailty of a 'peace' that has been dearly bought. The CNDP has been incorporated into the national army, and Nkunda's brutish successor, Bosco Ntaganda, appointed a general in the government army, despite being wanted by the International Criminal Court for war crimes, including conscripting child soldiers. 'We made a painful decision,' Kabila tells me. 'In Congo, peace must come before justice.'

Though there is little of either, Kabila has another ace up his sleeve. A $9 billion deal will give China a slice of Congo's vast reserves of copper, cobalt and other minerals, in return for building 2,400 miles of road, 2,000 miles of railway, 32 health centres and two universities. While this may not stop the fighting, Kabila calculates that the planned improvements to his country will enhance his personal prestige. The new infrastructure, to be concentrated in the eastern heartland where Kabila needs the votes, could be a boon to Congo's children.

Instead, it seems possible that the deal will mean more exploitation. Youngsters not signed up as soldiers are often requisitioned as miners, labouring for a pittance to dig the minerals, such as cassiterite (tin ore), that make warlords rich and fund Congo's endless conflict. A spokesman for the charity Global Witness says, 'You see kids of seven working long days in small tunnels.'

China's planned stake in the extractive industries has alarmed aid workers, who fear its dubious human rights record will make things worse. 'That would certainly be a concern,' says Daniel Large, the research director of the Africa Asia Centre at the School of Oriental and African Studies in London. 'Where you have weak regulation, Chinese companies are not unique in trying to get away with anything. But equally, you shouldn't have only negative expectations. If anything, you can argue this is welcome. Congo needs investment, and it's the first time a Chinese resource deal has had a social component, such as building schools.'

For decades the west has either violated Congo, in the case of the Belgian colonialists who inspired Joseph Conrad's *Heart of Darkness*, or averted its gaze from a land whose children are sacrificed to brutality and greed. British politicians, like their European counterparts, have promised to help, but their good intentions have faded into silence.

In the playground of the rehabilitation centre, the music group is singing. 'Les enfants réclament la paix dans leur pays. Toujours la paix (the children reclaim peace in their country. Always peace).' They have learnt to believe in a better tomorrow. But who, in Congo and the wider world, will justify their faith?

Names of the child soldiers have been changed
16 July 2009

⇨ The International Labour Organization (ILO) believes that up to 1.2 million children are trafficked annually all over the world. (page 1)

⇨ In 1989 the UN put together the Convention on the Rights of the Child, which outlined the right of children to be protected from economic exploitation, and also the right to be protected from having to perform jobs that could be hazardous to their health or wellbeing. (page 2)

⇨ Two-thirds of all children that are not going to school are girls. The work that they perform is often hardly visible, e.g. in one's own or someone else's household (domestic child labour). (page 5)

⇨ More than 200 million children worldwide are still in child labour and a staggering 115 million – at least – are subject to its worst forms. (page 6)

⇨ Most child labourers continue to work in agriculture (60 per cent). Only one in five working children is in paid employment. The overwhelming majority are unpaid family workers. (page 7)

⇨ Globally, there are now 30 million fewer working children than ten years ago. (page 9)

⇨ The emerging economies of Bangladesh, China, India, Nigeria and Pakistan are rated as the countries with most risk of human rights violations against underage workers in a new survey. (page 11)

⇨ Given its hidden nature, it is impossible to have reliable figures on how many children are globally exploited as domestic workers. According to the ILO, though, more girl-children under 16 are in domestic service than in any other category of child labour. (page 12)

⇨ Though a global report shows a modest decline in the rate of child labour, the International Labour Organization (ILO) has expressed doubt as to whether the goal of eliminating the menace by 2016 could be realised. (page 15)

⇨ Commercial sexual exploitation of children through prostitution is a global problem and is closely connected to child pornography and the trafficking of children for sexual purposes. Demand for sex with children may come from both local and foreign exploiters. (page 17)

⇨ Any child or young person may be at risk of sexual exploitation, regardless of their family background or other circumstances. This includes boys and young men as well as girls and young women. (page 20)

⇨ Because of the grooming methods used by their abusers, it is very common for children and young people who are sexually exploited not to recognise that they are being abused. (page 23)

⇨ Trafficked and exploited children will all suffer from a form of post-traumatic stress relating to their sense of powerlessness and the degree of violence they experienced at the hands of their traffickers, which can be extreme. (page 29)

⇨ People who buy pirate DVDs and roses from street vendors, smoke home-grown cannabis, give money to child beggars and use prostitutes may be supporting what the United Nations has described as 'a modern day slave trade', says research published by ECPAT. (page 30)

⇨ Less than half of prosecutions for human trafficking offences, including the exploitation of children for sex or crime, result in a conviction. (page 31)

⇨ Africa has the largest number of child soldiers. Child soldiers are being used in armed conflict in Central African Republic, Chad, Democratic Republic of Congo, Somalia and Sudan. (page 33)

⇨ There are at least 300,000 child soldiers in the world today. One in three is a girl. (page 35)

⇨ About 31,000 children have been demobilised from Congo's battlefields since 1999, but at least 8,000 are still being used as combatants, porters and sex slaves. (page 37)

Boycott

A form of activism in which consumers refuse to buy a product or use a service to protest against unethical practices by the manufacturer/provider.

Child exploitation

Child exploitation is a broad term which includes forced or dangerous labour, child trafficking and child prostitution. The term is used to refer to situations where children are abused – physically, verbally or sexually – or when they are submitted to unsatisfactory conditions as part of their forced or voluntary employment.

Child labour

There is no universally-accepted definition of child labour. However, it might generally be said to be work for children that harms or exploits them in some way (physically, mentally, morally, or by blocking access to education). According to the International Labour Organization, more than 200 million children worldwide are still in child labour and 115 million at least are subject to its worst forms.

Commercial sexual exploitation of children

The Declaration and Agenda for Action against Commercial Sexual Exploitation of Children defines this as 'a fundamental violation of children's rights. It comprises sexual abuse by the adult and remuneration in cash or kind to the child or a third person or persons. The child is treated as a sexual object and a commercial object. The commercial sexual exploitation of children constitutes a form of coercion and violence against children, and amounts to forced labour and a contemporary form of slavery'. Commercial sexual exploitation of children may take the form of child abuse through the prostitution of children; using children to create images of child sex abuse (child 'pornography'); providing children to visitors from overseas for the purpose of sexual abuse (child sex tourism), and child marriage where a child is used for sexual purposes in exchange for goods or services. Children who are sexually exploited in these ways may have been trafficked from another country for that purpose.

Child soldiers

A child soldier is a person under the age of 18 associated with an armed force or group, who has been recruited or used by an armed group in any capacity. This includes children, both boys and girls, used as fighters, cooks, porters, spies, domestic servants or for sexual purposes. It does not only refer to a child who is taking, or has taken, a direct part in hostilities. Child soldiers may be volunteers, or they may have been abducted, forced or coerced into their position by the armed group with which they are associated.

Child trafficking

'Trafficking' is not the same as 'people smuggling', where immigrants and asylum seekers pay people to help them enter another country illegally. Victims of trafficking are coerced or deceived by the person arranging their relocation. On arrival in the country of destination, a trafficked child is denied their human rights and forced into exploitation by the trafficker or person into whose control they are delivered.

DDR

This abbreviation stands for Disarmament, Demobilisation and Reintegration. It refers to the programmes which are in place in some regions to help rehabilitate child soldiers: they are rescued from the armed groups they are associated with, helped to deal with psychological damage arising from their traumatic experiences and hopefully are then able to be reintegrated into their communities.

Debt bondage

Also called bonded labour, this means that an individual is forced to pay off a debt by working for the person to whom they owe money. Where someone is made to work for little or no pay, or for a far longer period than it would take to pay their debt, this can be seen as a form of modern-day slavery. In some situations, whole families, including children, can be held in bonded labour, or children can be forced to work on behalf of another family member who owes money.

Domestic labour

Work which takes place in the home: for example, minding children, cooking, cleaning.

Sweatshop

A hazardous or exploitative working environment, where employees may work long hours for very low pay. Employers often violate legal requirements regarding workers' rights, such as minimum pay regulations.

abuse
  trafficked children 29
  see also sexual exploitation
Africa, child soldiers 33, 37–9
age
  child soldiers 33–4
  and definitions of children 3, 16
  of sexual consent 16
Asia, child soldiers 33

Bolivia, child labour 9–10
boycotts, effect on child labour 13

Cambodia, child labour 9
child exploitation
  definition 1
  reasons for 2
child labour 1–15
  consumer influence 13–14
  definitions 3
  domestic labour 12
  and education 4–5
  elimination 2, 4–5, 7–8, 15
  hazards 4, 12
  numbers of child labourers 3–4, 6–7
  reasons for 5, 12
Child Labour Index 11
child marriage 19
child pornography 17–18
child prostitution 17, 24–6
child sex tourism 18–19
child sexual exploitation *see* sexual exploitation
child soldiers 32–9
  numbers 32–3
  punishment 34
  rehabilitation 36, 37–9
child trafficking *see* trafficking
children
  definition of 3, 16
  missing education 5, 14
China, child labour 11
commercial sexual exploitation 16–31
  definition 16
Congo, child soldiers 37–9
consent, age of 16
consumer influence
  and child labour 13–14
  and child trafficking 30
Convention on the Rights of the Child 2
convictions for child trafficking 31
cotton industry and child labour 13–14
crime and sexual exploitation 22

discrimination and child trafficking 28
domestic labour 12

early marriage 19

education
  and child trafficking 28
  and children in the cotton industry 14
  and elimination of child labour 4–5
  girls 5
  importance of 4
  and poverty 4
emerging economies and child labour 11
'End Child Exploitation' campaign 2
ethical consumption 13
Europe, child soldiers 33

families, impact of child sexual exploitation 23

gender and child labour 5, 6
girls
  as child soldiers 32, 35–6
  and education 5
  as victims of trafficking 28
Global Action Plan (ILO) 7
grooming 21, 25

health issues, child soldiers 36

ILO *see* International Labour Organization
India, child labour 11
International Labour Organization (ILO) 2, 7–8
  definition of child labour 3
  Global Action Plan 7
  report on child labour 15
International Programme on the Elimination of Child Labour (IPEC) 7
Internet and child pornography 18

Latin America, child soldiers 33

Mali, child labour 10
marriage, children 19
Middle East, child soldiers 33
motherhood, girl soldiers 36

neglect, trafficked children 29

Palermo Protocol 2, 27
parents, impact of children's sexual exploitation 23
physical abuse, trafficked children 29
pornography 17–18
poverty
  and child labour 4
  and child trafficking 27
prosecutions for child trafficking 31
prostitution 17, 24–6
Protection of Children from Sexual Exploitation in Travel and Tourism, Code of Conduct 19
psychological harm, trafficked children 29

risks of child labour 4, 12

'School is the best place to work' campaign 5
sex tourism 18–19
sexual consent, age of 16
sexual exploitation 16–31
  case study 24–6
  impacts on children 22–3
  perpetrators 20–21
soldiers, child 32–9

tourism, sex 18–19
trafficking 27–31

definition 1
impact on children 29
low conviction rate 31
in UK 27–9, 30, 31

UK
  child exploitation 1–2
  trafficked children 27–9, 30, 31
UN Convention on the Rights of the Child 2
UNICEF 'End Child Exploitation' campaign 2

ACKNOWLEDGEMENTS

The publisher is grateful for permission to reproduce the following material.

While every care has been taken to trace and acknowledge copyright, the publisher tenders its apology for any accidental infringement or where copyright has proved untraceable. The publisher would be pleased to come to a suitable arrangement in any such case with the rightful owner.

Chapter One: Child Labour

Child exploitation, © Action on Child Exploitation, Frequently asked questions about child labour, © Stop Child Labour, Facts on child labour 2010, © 2010 International Labour Organization, The face of child labour from Africa to Asia and the Americas, © 2010 International Labour Organization, Emerging economies 'worst for child labour risk', © Institute of Risk Management, Domestic labour, © 2010 International Labour Organization, The consumer and child labour, © Stop Child Labour, ILO fears the goal of eliminating child labour by 2016 may not be reached, © Ghana News Agency.

Chapter Two: Commercial Sexual Exploitation

The commercial sexual exploitation of children, © ECPAT, Safeguarding children and young people from sexual exploitation, © Crown copyright is reproduced with the permission of Her Majesty's Stationery Office, 'They like us naïve': how teenage girls are groomed for a life of prostitution by UK gangs, © The Independent, Trafficked and exploited children, © London Child Protection Committee, Fifth of Britons unknowingly aid child trafficking, according to survey, © Guardian News and Media Limited 2010, Concerns raised over low number of convictions for child trafficking, © Children & Young People Now.

Chapter Three: Child Soldiers

Fighting isn't just for boys: girls go to war, © Women's Refugee Commission 2009, Rebuilding the lives of Congo's child soldiers, © Telegraph Media Group Limited 2010.

Illustrations

Pages 1, 24, 32, 39: Simon Kneebone; pages 6, 30, 35: Angelo Madrid; pages 10, 21: Bev Aisbett; pages 14, 31, 36: Don Hatcher.

Cover photography

Left: © Supreet Vaid. Centre: © Aurileide Alves. Right: © John Hughes.

Additional acknowledgements

Additional editorial by Carolyn Kirby on behalf of Independence.

And with thanks to the Independence team: Mary Chapman, Sandra Dennis and Jan Sunderland.

Lisa Firth
Cambridge
January, 2011

The following tasks aim to help you think through the issues surrounding child exploitation and provide a better understanding of the topic.

1 Pick out some of the statistics given in *Facts on child labour 2010* on pages 6–8 and represent them in the form of a graph such as a bar or pie chart. Do you feel the figures have a greater impact when viewed in this format?

2 Find out about the use of child labour in the UK during a historical period of your choosing. What kinds of work were children expected to do? What hazards existed for working children? How much would they have been paid? Write an article exploring your findings.

3 Read Leap's story in *The face of child labour from Africa to Asia and the Americas* on page 9. Write a stream of consciousness monologue from Leap's point of view over the course of one day, and then a monologue from the viewpoint of an average 10-year-old girl here in the UK, considering how their experiences of life and of childhood are worlds apart.

4 Read *The consumer and child labour* on pages 13–14. Select some high-street chains and brands of which you are aware and use the Internet to research their policies regarding ethical production practices. Use the company's own site as well as other sites such as newspaper archives and charity or lobby group websites. Are the items available to buy on British high streets produced ethically? Have any producers used sweatshop or child labour in the past, and do any continue to do so? Write a summary of your findings.

5 Read 'Oliver Twist' by Charles Dickens and write a review, focusing on the type of world Oliver inhabits and its attitude to children and childhood.

6 Find out how Amnesty International works to help victims of human rights abuses. What work do they do for and with exploited children and young people?

7 'This house believes that child labour is a tragic but necessary economic evil which enables emerging economies to progress and the very poorest to survive.' Debate this motion as a class, with one group arguing in favour and the other against.

8 Read the section of *The consumer and child labour* called 'Should we boycott?' (on page 13). Do you agree with this view that boycotts are counter-productive? How would you feel if you discovered one of your favourite brands was produced using child labour – would you want to stop buying it? Discuss your views with a partner.

9 Read *'They like us naïve': how teenage girls are groomed for a life of prostitution by UK gangs* on pages 24–26. Using information from the articles in 'Chapter Two: Commercial Sexual Exploitation', create an illustrated booklet advising girls and young women about how to keep themselves and their friends safe from potential 'groomers'.

10 Read *Fifth of Britons unknowingly aid child trafficking, according to survey* on page 30. Create a hard-hitting poster designed to raise public awareness of this issue, to be displayed near places where pirate DVD sellers are known to operate.

11 Watch the 15-rated film 'Blood Diamond' (WARNING: contains violent scenes which some may find harrowing). How does it explore the issue of child soldiers through the experiences of the character Dia? Write a review.

12 Find out about Red Hand Day. What is it, when and why is it observed? How could you participate in or promote the campaign?

13 Read 'A Long Way Gone: Memoirs of a Boy Soldier' by Ishmael Beah and write a summary of its portrayal of the life of a child soldier.

14 Look at the map on page 34. Choose one of the shaded countries and do some research into the conflicts taking place there, and the participating armed groups which use child soldiers. Using your research, create a presentation on the plight of child soldiers in this country. You could include personal stories and photographs of some of the children involved.